BBC

VOLUME 4

JOSHUA JUDGES and RUTH

Barbara P. Ferguson

ABINGDON PRESS
Nashville

D1166878

JOSHUA, JUDGES, AND RUTH

Copyright © 1988 by Graded Press

This book is printed on recycled, acid-free paper.

Library of Congress Cataloging-in-Publication Data

Cokesbury basic Bible commentary.
     Basic Bible commentary / by Linda B. Hinton . . . [et al.].
        p.   cm.
     Originally published: Cokesbury basic Bible commentary. Nashville: Graded Press, c 1988.
     ISBN 0-687-02620-2 (pbk. : v. 1 : alk. paper)
     1. Bible—Commentaries.   I. Hinton, Linda B.   II. Title.
[BS491.2.C65 1994]
220.7—dc20   94-10965
                                                                                  CIP

ISBN 0-687-02623-7 (v. 4, Joshua–Ruth)
ISBN 0-687-02620-2 (v. 1, Genesis)
ISBN 0-687-02621-0 (v. 2, Exodus–Leviticus)
ISBN 0-687-02622-9 (v. 3, Numbers–Deuteronomy)
ISBN 0-687-02624-5 (v. 5, 1–2 Samuel)
ISBN 0-687-02625-3 (v. 6, 1–2 Kings)
ISBN 0-687-02626-1 (v. 7, 2 Chronicles)
ISBN 0-687-02627-X (v. 8, Ezra–Esther)
ISBN 0-687-02628-8 (v. 9, Job)
ISBN 0-687-02629-6 (v. 10, Psalms)
ISBN 0-687-02630-X (v. 11, Proverbs–Song of Solomon)
ISBN 0-687-02631-8 (v. 12, Isaiah)
ISBN 0-687-02632-6 (v. 13, Jeremiah–Lamentation)
ISBN 0-687-02633-4 (v. 14, Ezekiel–Daniel)
ISBN 0-687-02634-2 (v. 15, Hosea–Jonah)
ISBN 0-687-02635-0 (v. 16, Micah–Malachi)
ISBN 0-687-02636-9 (v. 17, Matthew)
ISBN 0-687-02637-7 (v. 18, Mark)
ISBN 0-687-02638-5 (v. 19, Luke)
ISBN 0-687-02639-3 (v. 20, John)
ISBN 0-687-02640-7 (v. 21, Acts)
ISBN 0-687-02642-3 (v. 22, Romans)
ISBN 0-687-02643-1 (v. 23, 1–2 Corinthians)
ISBN 0-687-02644-X (v. 24, Galatians–Ephesians)
ISBN 0-687-02645-8 (v. 25, Philippians–2 Thessalonians)
ISBN 0-687-02646-6 (v. 26, 1 Timothy–Philemon)
ISBN 0-687-02647-4 (v. 27, Hebrews)
ISBN 0-687-02648-2 (v. 28, James–Jude)
ISBN 0-687-02649-0 (v. 29, Revelation)
ISBN 0-687-02650-4 (complete set of 29 vols.)

99 00 01 02 03—10 9 8 7 6 5 4 3

MANUFACTURED IN THE UNITED STATES OF AMERICA

Contents

Outline of Joshua, Judges, and Ruth

Joshua

I. The Conquest of Canaan (1:1–12:24)
  A. Preparations (1:1–2:24)
    1. Joshua assumes command (1:1-11)
    2. The Transjordan tribes pledge aid (1:12-18)
    3. The spies (2:1-24)
  B. Crossing the Jordan (3:1–5:15)
    1. God promises help (3:1-13)
    2. The crossing (3:14–4:8)
    3. The crossing completed (4:9-5:1)
    4. In camp at Gilgal (5:2-15)
  C. Attacks on Jericho and Ai (6:1–8:35)
    1. Preparations (6:1-7)
    2. The fall of Jericho (6:8-21)
    3. Rahab spared (6:22-27)
    4. First attack on Ai fails (7:1-26)
    5. Victory at Ai (8:1-35)
  D. Continued conquest (9:1-12:24)
    1. Treaty with Gibeonites (9:1-27)
    2. Southern campaigns (10:1-43)
    3. Northern campaigns (11:1-23)
    4. Conclusion (12:1-24)
II. After the Conquest (13:1–24:33)
  A. Distribution of the land (13:1–21:45)
    1. Land still unconquered (13:1-7)
    2. Inheritance of the Transjordan Tribes (13:8-33)
    3. Division Among Remaining Tribes (14:1–19:51)
    4. Special cities and conclusion (20:1–21:45)

B. Joshua's last days (22:1–24:33)
   1. Departure of Transjordan tribes (22:1-34)
   2. Farewell address (23:1-16)
   3. Covenant at Shechem (24:1-28)
   4. Three burials (24:29-33)

Judges

I. Review of the Conquest (1:1–3:6)
   A. Conquest and settlement (1:1–2:5)
      1. Many a battle (1:1-36)
      2. Departure from Gilgal (2:1-5)
   B. Introduction to the Judges (2:6–3:6)
      1. Joshua dies (2:6-10)
      2. Israel's infidelity (2:11-23)
      3. Israel among the nations (3:1-6)
II. Stories of the Judges (3:7–16:31)
   A. Three early Judges (3:7-31)
      1. Othniel (3:7-11)
      2. Ehud (3:12-30)
      3. Shamgar (3:31)
   B. Deborah and Barak (4:1–5:31)
      1. The oppression (4:1-3)
      2. Deborah and Barak plan (4:4-9)
      3. The victory (4:10-24)
      4. The song of Deborah (5:1-31)

Ruth

I. Problem and Initial Solution (1:1–2:23)
  A. Moab (1:1-18)
  B. Bethlehem (1:19-22)
  C. Gleaning (2:1-23)
II. A Happy Ending (3:1–4:22)
  A. Naomi's plan (3:1-18)
  B. A slight hitch (4:1-12)
  C. Conclusion (4:13-22)

Introduction to Joshua

The sixth book of our Bible is named for Joshua, the central figure in its story. That story is the story of Israel's conquest of Canaan. Joshua is a great leader in these events, yet he is not a hero in the usual sense. Joshua does not accomplish great deeds by his own ability. Instead, Joshua appears as God's instrument. It is God who is the real hero here.

Jews have traditionally classed Joshua as the first of the books called the Former Prophets (Joshua–2 Kings). These are not prophetic books as we know them, but they received the name for two reasons: (1) After a time, people began to call all great religious leaders *prophets*, and (2) these books reflect a prophetic view of history.

Christians, on the other hand, usually class Joshua as a historical book, because Joshua tells the history of Israel's conquest and settlement of the Promised Land. More than that, though, this book tells of God's action in and through specific historical events. Joshua gives us both history and a religious interpretation of that history.

Relationship to Other Biblical Books

The book of Joshua stands as an essential part of the whole historical sequence sweeping from Genesis to Nehemiah. As one portion of the ongoing story of God's action in Israel's history, Joshua has strong ties to many biblical books. In Joshua we see God's fulfillment of the Genesis promises to Abraham. Joshua carries forth the themes of law and covenant so basic to the book of

Exodus. Sometimes the man Joshua even appears as a parallel to the Exodus leader, Moses. The Psalms often mention the conquest story in poetic praise of God for mighty acts. As mentioned before, Joshua shares a religious viewpoint with many of the prophets. The book has its closest ties, however, with a literary unit that runs from Deuteronomy through Second Kings. Style and theology show that this whole epic was probably written by one school of writers who maintained a standard outlook and formula for expression. So, Joshua does not stand alone; it is part of a much larger biblical picture.

Authorship

Literary and theological evidence shows that someone (probably just one person) from the Deuteronomy-Second Kings school composed the final version of Joshua. We do not know this author's name. Instead, for convenience, we usually call any writer from this school "D," and say Joshua was written by D. It's not quite that simple, however. The book is now a well-organized whole, but there are signs that the author used many older sources for his work. He has blended together many stories, some of them ancient tribal traditions whose originators are unknown. This blending has left a few contradictions. For instance in 4:8, twelve stones are carried out of the Jordan. But in 4:9, twelve stones are set up in the river. Either way, the writer still makes his point. His concern to glorify God comes through.

Theology

The book of Joshua shows us a God of unlimited power, justice, and grace. God acts in historical events of this world. Israel is God's chosen instrument in the world. Obedience to God's command gives Israel success; disobedience brings failure. God's promises are true and worthy of trust. The covenant is both God's gracious gift and Israel's moral responsibility.

For special reasons, God wants Israel to possess the

land of Canaan. God has promised it and works with the faithful people to bring this about. The conquest is thus a gift, not Joshua's nor Israel's achievement. God's will for the people is freedom and self-determination, and God follows through to give Israel a homeland.

Most of us probably find little quarrel with such a theology. Yet underneath there are some problems. One has been the over-simplification of the "obedience equals success" theory. Some have taken this belief to mean that (1) we can win God's favor by good works, or (2) that every misfortune is proof of sin. Seeing these problems, many have supposed that the writer was a shallow thinker. Perhaps he had not even considered the problem of innocent suffering. So they have written him off. But perhaps the writer was speaking only of the nation's long-term well-being, not of individual short-term events.

Another problem that often bothers readers of Joshua is the picture they see of God as a God of violence and bloodshed, a God who seems to advocate pure mayhem if it suits the divine purposes. Since this is not the God we know through Jesus, many simply dismiss Joshua as primitive religious fanaticism. Others suggest that Israel's religious understanding had just not developed far enough to see God as a God of consistent love toward everyone. But we must remember that peace was always offered before a town was destroyed. The writer may actually be expressing a much deeper thought: that this God is one who works through the people and institutions of this world as they are, good or evil. God uses war, even though it is evil, because God works with what is here, not what we might wish were here.

Dates

In Joshua there are two dates to consider: the date of the events and the date when the writer wrote them down.

The date of the events themselves is fairly clear. After

the Exodus from Egypt and the wilderness wanderings, Israel finally established a home in Canaan. This probably happened in the late thirteenth century B.C.

The date of writing is more complex. We cannot tell how old the ancient sources may be. Scholars are fairly sure, however, that the final writing took place in the sixth or seventh century B.C. Most place it during the Exile (587-538 B.C.). Some commentators place the writing just before the fall of Jerusalem in 587 B.C. In either case we find that someone living 600 to 700 years after the event has determined to tie this story together, to preserve his nation's history, and to interpret that history in the light of faith.

Historical Value

With such a time lapse between the events and the final book we might expect some information gaps, some fuzziness on details. And we do find them in Joshua. So how much historical fact can we expect from this book? Our answer, given the circumstances, is: a surprising amount. Because of information from Judges 1 and other sources, scholars formerly thought that the conquest was really a slow infiltration, with each tribe working more or less alone. Some tribes may not even have left Canaan for Egypt at all. This is very different from the concentrated campaigns we see in Joshua. So scholars supposed that Joshua was an idealized version of the process. More recent archeological evidence, however, has shown a massive destruction of Canaanite cites in the thirteenth century. It appears that a concerted effort may have occurred and that Joshua may well be more accurate than previously assumed. For now, we cannot know exactly how quickly or how closely the tribes worked. That need not, however, keep us from understanding the author's main point: the saving, freeing action of God in the history of a faithful, obedient people.

Joshua 1–2

Introduction to These Chapters

From the very first verse the author makes it clear that the book of Joshua is a continuation of Israel's great historical narrative. He takes up precisely where the book of Deuteronomy ends, with the death of Moses. Moses has led the people to God's promised land. Now the conquest of that land is about to begin.

In the same first verse the author brings in the name of Joshua. Joshua is to take up where Moses left off. Here and in the following ten verses is the author's introduction. It is an introduction that assures a smooth transition from the last book to this one. In it the author shows that human leadership is changing, but God's purposes and position of command are not.

Following the introduction we find some ancient traditions concerning the conquest itself, including the story of a specific incident through which God worked to help Israel toward its first victory. Throughout these verses, as throughout the book, God is at the center. It is God who promises, commands, and aids the people. Joshua is God's instrument for the task at hand.

Here is an outline of these chapters.
I. Joshua Assumes Command (1:1-11)
II. The Transjordan Tribes Pledge Aid (1:12-18)
III. The Spies (2:1-24)

Joshua Assumes Command (1:1-11)

After their escape from Egypt, the Israelites had wandered in the wilderness (or desert) areas south of Palestine, waiting for the time when they could enter the Promised Land. This Promised Land was the land of Canaan, or Palestine. It lay on the land bridge between Asia and Africa. The area is split north to south by the Jordan River. To the east of the Jordan is a plateau. To the west there is a central mountain range running north and south, then some foothills, and finally a plain that continues west to the Mediterranean Sea. (See the map on page 155.) The people of Israel have come around Canaan's southern borders to the east bank of the Jordan. Across the river lies the bulk of their Promised Land. But it is already occupied. They will have to conquer the land.

They have come at a good time, however. The Hittite empire that previously controlled the area has crumbled. Canaan's towns are not effectively joined or systematically defended.

Israel's leader, Moses, has died. The mantle of leadership passes to his assistant, Joshua. It is Joshua who will now serve as God's instrument to fulfill the promise of a homeland. God gives instruction and encouragement. Then Joshua commands the people to prepare for the invasion.

Joshua means *Yahweh (God) is salvation.* Joshua is sometimes called *Hoshea* instead. This is the same Joshua who assisted Moses in the wilderness and who went with the twelve spies into Canaan (Numbers 13:8; 14:6, 38). Of those twelve only Joshua and Caleb believed that the land could be conquered.

Nun is Joshua's father. Nothing is known of Nun except that he was a member of the tribe of Ephraim. Some scholars believe that Nun was actually a sub-tribe rather than an individual.

Joshua is described as the *assistant* (NRSV) or *aide* (NIV) to Moses.

Lebanon is the range of mountains to the north of Palestine. The *Euphrates* is a river far to the northeast, and the *great sea* is the Mediterranean.

The *Hittites* were a people from the north who had built a large empire that included much of Palestine. Some Hittites probably still lived in the area, and the old empire was still called the land of the Hittites.

The boundaries of the Promised Land (verse 4) included a territory much larger than any that Israel ever actually controlled. They reflect, however, the hope that Israel would someday be a large, strong nation.

God offers strength on condition that the people be steadfast, remain faithful, and take care to obey the *Book of the Law* (verse 8). This book is evidently the law as written in the Book of Deuteronomy. Here we see the writer's special concern with this law.

The Jordan River split Palestine north to south. Israel was camped on the east side of the Jordan. Most of the Promised Land lay west of the Jordan.

The Transjordan Tribes Pledge Aid (1:12-18)

Now Joshua speaks particularly to three groups: the Reubenites, the Gadites, and the half-tribe of Manasseh. He specifically reminds them of Moses' command to join the other tribes in conquering Canaan. He does this because, as we know looking back, these tribes settled on the east bank of the Jordan. They already had, or were near, their land. It would be tempting for them to just settle down and let the rest of Israel take care of itself. The fact that these tribes' families remained on the east bank suggests that perhaps they already were rather established. Yet at God's command they joined the others in conquering the land to the west. From the conquest to the writer's own time, staying together has been essential for Israel's survival.

The tribe of Manasseh eventually settled partly on the east and partly on the west of the Jordan. Joshua here

14

addresses the eastern part of the tribe. The use of the term *half-tribe* shows that the writer was speaking from hindsight.

The Spies (2:1-24)

Here is the story of one incident that helped make the conquest possible. In preparation for the invasion, Joshua sends two spies to Jericho so he may know just what Israel is up against. They enter the city and stop at the house of Rahab. She tells them that the Canaanites fear an Israelite invasion. Then she hides them and helps them escape. In return for her help and silence, the spies agree to protect her and her household when Israel attacks the city.

Shittim is the place where Israel is camped on the east bank of the Jordan. It lies across the river from Jericho.

Rahab was a prostitute. Strictly speaking, the men should not have been associating with her. All the same, she was one who could be expected to know about prevailing attitudes and who might not be an especially loyal citizen. People might not notice the comings and goings of strangers in such a house. So Rahab was a fairly safe person for the spies to contact.

Conditions could be crowded inside a walled city. Archeology has uncovered many a house built right against the wall, using the city wall as part of the house. Thus, Rahab had a window on the outer wall. It proved a handy escape route for the spies.

§ § § § § § §

The Message of Joshua 1–2

In even this short passage we find many of the Deuteronomists' basic ideas. We see a God active in history, a God who commands and leads the people, a God who is working to fulfill the promises made to Israel. We see God offering help and strength from the very onset of a difficult struggle. But God's help is conditional; it depends on the people's faithfulness and obedience to the law. The people's success also depends upon their working together. The achievement of good is a cooperative process. It requires cooperation of the people with each other and with God. Only thus can a strong, successful nation be formed and endure.

To us in our time this passage reiterates a timeless biblical message. The almighty God cares for us, will strengthen and guide us, and will fulfill the promises made to us. We, however, bear a part of the responsibility for our own success. We must obey God and work cooperatively with others. God gives the law, not simply to assert authority, but to guide us and to keep us in fellowship with God. If we disobey, we will be going against the grain of life, so we can only fall into difficulty and failure. The tragic stories of many individuals and nations who have made their own rules attest to this wisdom from the ancient past.

§ § § § § § §

Introduction to These Chapters

Now Israel is ready to take the big step. The people will cross the Jordan and invade the land of Canaan. The crossing itself is a miraculous one, a never-to-be-forgotten event. God's power continues to work in this latest stage of the people's struggle for freedom. God is still acting to fulfill the promise.

These chapters, like the previous ones, contain traces of many traditions. The author has skillfully joined them to tell as completely as possible the story of one of the greatest events in Israel's history.

Like all of Joshua, however, this is more than a story. As striking as the events themselves is the attitude the author conveys. At each step we see the people's reverence, obedience, and worship. The author is very concerned that we recognize the importance of these attitudes. This is the work of a person who is trying to preserve and enhance his own people's reverence and faith.

We can see in these chapters some of the writer's other concerns, too. We will note his interest in ritual, his interest in preserving and magnifying liturgical forms, his concern for remembrance of historical events and God's actions in them, and his special interest in the law. The writer wants us to know how Israel came into possession of the land, but he also wants us to learn a religious outlook on all of history. He wants us to see the

power and love of God at work in the lives of the chosen
people.

Here is an outline of chapters 3–5.
  I. God Promises Help (3:1-13)
 II. The Crossing (3:14–4:8)
III. The Crossing Completed (4:9–5:1)
IV. In Camp at Gilgal (5:2-15)

God Promises Help (3:1-13)

In these verses the people prepare to cross the Jordan.
Joshua commands them to break camp and move
forward. Then he outlines what will be happening. He
explains that God is about to do a mighty act. This
miracle will prove God's power and trustworthiness.
Priests carrying the ark of the covenant will lead the
people across the river. But it is the power of God that
will make the difficult crossing possible.

We learn here that the Shittim camp is not on the river
but slightly to the east. The people must move and set up
camp again on the river bank.

In 1:11 Joshua said that in *three days* the people would
cross the Jordan. The spies were gone *three days* (2:22).
Now the people camp at the Jordan *three days*. Perhaps
these are the same three days that the spies were gone, or
perhaps we have here several stories, all of which are
tied together with the idea of a three-day wait.

The *ark of the covenant* was the sacred box that held the
Law. It represented God's powerful presence among the
people. It also symbolized God's special covenant
relationship with Israel and reminded the tribes of their
mutual bond to each other within that covenant. Note the
central place the ark takes in the miraculous crossing.
The writer's special concern with the law puts it right in
the forefront; it is an instrument of God's freeing power.

Two thousand cubits (NRSV) is about *1,000 yards* (NIV).
The need for such space shows the power of God. One

18   JOSHUA, JUDGES, AND RUTH

must not get too close to sacred objects. The people must show reverence and awe in the presence of the almighty God.

Joshua's brief command to *sanctify yourselves* again shows the writer's interest in liturgical purity and his concern for that attitude of worship and reverence. This invasion is not just a military campaign; it is a highly significant religious experience. The people must prepare themselves spiritually and ritually for it.

Various ethnic groups living in Canaan at the time included Canaanites, Hittites, Hivites, Perizzites, Girgashites, Amorites, and Jebusites.

The phrase LORD *of all the earth* provides yet another emphasis upon God's power. It is an invitation to awe and reverence.

The Crossing (3:14–4:8)

The actual crossing of the Jordan parallels the crossing of the Red Sea. The deep waters of the Jordan are held back by God's power. The people can cross over on dry land. There are two striking differences, however. One is that now the enemy is before Israel, not behind. The other is that priests and the ark now play major parts in the event. Again, the writer's concern with ritual and law comes through.

It is April, the time when melting snow from the mountains floods the Jordan. The crossing would be especially difficult at this time. Therefore, the miracle of God's holding back the water is all the greater. One "natural" cause for the river's damming has been known to occur. That is a mild earthquake, which is not uncommon in the area. Such a quake could send debris into the river, diverting or stopping the flow for a time.

Adam is Adamah, a town upriver on the Jordan.

Zarethan is a city about twelve miles north of Adamah. It would not be exactly beside Adamah. There are some translation problems here, but the point seems to be that the water was dammed for some distance up the river.

The *sea of the Arabah* is the Dead Sea.

A representative of each tribe participates in the event and in its memorial *(twelve men)*. Again we see the emphasis upon unity—all the tribes have a part. The men are to take *twelve stones* to their next campsite. This is an act of reverence and a historical reminder. Thus the writer reinforces the importance of this miraculous event and the necessity of remembering God's act here at the Jordan.

The Crossing Completed (4:9–5:1)

The last of the people cross the Jordan River, the priests come out of the water with the ark, and the waters return to normal. The leaders of Canaan, hearing of the miracle, quake in fear because they know that God is with Israel.

The material contains a mixture of traditions. The message of God's power, however, comes through. At each step God commands, and Joshua obeys. God has made a great miracle. Not only Israel, but pagan peoples must recognize God's overwhelming might.

In verse 11 we note that the priests leave the river. In verse 17 Joshua commands the priests to come up out of the river. Here is another example of two traditions that have been brought together. The story is basically the same, but small details differ or are repeated.

In verse 9 Joshua sets up twelve stones in the Jordan. In verse 20 twelve stones are taken out of the Jordan. Perhaps Joshua prepared two memorials of the crossing. More likely, however, these are two different traditions. The point of each is the same: to recognize God's greatness and to remember it. *What do these stones mean?* Again the writer pounds away at the theme of remembrance.

The exact location of Gilgal is debated. However, it was certainly quite close to Jericho. *Gilgal* means *circle*. Perhaps a circle of twelve ceremonial stones gave it its name. The Israelites camped at Gilgal and used it as a major base for their invasion.

In Camp at Gilgal (5:2-15)

The people camp at Gilgal. The writer's concern for ritual purity appears strongly in these verses. All must be spiritually right before the conquest can begin. So the people observe two very important Jewish rituals, circumcision and Passover. Both rituals serve to bind together the disparate tribes, and both offer worship and obedience to God.

Circumcision is cutting the foreskin from the male genital organ. Other groups practiced circumcision, but in Israel it carried special significance. Circumcision was a sign of membership in God's chosen people. It was also a sign of obedience, a purification rite, and a symbol of God's covenant with the people (see Genesis 17:9-14).

The writer has difficulty explaining why the men are being circumcised. In verse 2 Joshua is told to *circumcise the Israelites again* (NIV) or *a second time* (NRSV), but in verses 4-7 the writer explains that actually none of the boys born in the wilderness had been circumcised. Again, there were probably two traditions to explain a strong memory of circumcision rites at Gilgal. One other explanation exists: that some groups had not gone down into Egypt. When they joined the others, all who were uncircumcised were thus initiated, so that the common bond might be maintained and reinforced.

The name *Gilgal* is related to the Hebrew word *roll*. The writer uses the name of the place to emphasize the purifying aspects of the circumcision rite. God rolls away sin.

Passover celebrates the Exodus from Egypt, so it fits in quite well with the second crossing of a great water. The feast uses the last of the *manna*, the miraculous food God provided in the wilderness. On the next day unleavened cakes can be made of grain from the Promised Land itself.

When Joshua encounters God's representative, he must do just as Moses did at the burning bush: He must take off his shoes as a sign that this is an experience with the holy.

§ § § § § § §

The Message of Joshua 3–5

The message of the crossing is simple enough: God has unlimited power. God cares for the people, and will help them if they will remain obedient and reverent. Ritual is an important element of that obedience and reverence. Historical memories are also important because they remind us of God's great acts in the past and inspire awe, trust, and reverence in the present. Both remembrance and ritual help bind us to our fellow believers.

We today sometimes forget the vital role ritual can play in keeping us aware of God's greatness and trustworthiness. Certainly, ritual can be empty show. But if it is entered into with the heart, ritual can strengthen our faith. It can bind us in more trusting, more obedient fellowship with the almighty, loving God and with God's children.

§ § § § § § §

Joshua 6–8

Introduction to These Chapters

Now the conquest begins. These chapters chronicle the first two battles, those at Jericho and Ai. The well-known battle of Jericho was a tremendous success. The battle at Ai was a very different story—a story of sin and discovery, and a story of defeat and eventual victory.

The material in these chapters comes from several different sources, some of them probably quite ancient. We find here many double versions of events. Sometimes these versions do not agree in every detail. Some stories may have become blurred or confused by age, yet they carry important memories of God's action in a crucial era of Israel's life. These the author has woven into a powerful narrative of both history and faith.

The author's main points remain as in previous passages: God's almighty power and the importance of obedience.

Here is an outline of chapters 6–8.
I. Preparations (6:1-7)
II. The Fall of Jericho (6:8-21)
III. Rahab Spared (6:22-27)
IV. First Attack on Ai Fails (7:1-26)
V. Victory at Ai (8:1-35)

Preparations (6:1-7)

God commands the people to march around Jericho on seven consecutive days. What a strange way to attack a city! Yet Joshua obeys in every detail. The priests and the ark take their central place in the procession. On the seventh day, to horns and shouts, the city will fall.

The liturgical symbols of priests and ark continue to represent the presence of God's power. The writer's interest in worship and ritual keep these factors at the center of action throughout the conquest.

The passage speaks of seven days, seven priests, seven trumpets, and seven trips on the seventh day. The emphasis on seven probably comes from the writer's concern for the sabbath (seventh). It is another detail that shows the importance of religious tradition.

The ram's horn is another liturgical symbol. It is used in Jewish worship to this day.

Encircling the city could be a way of laying claim to territory. By tracing its borders the people stated that they claimed all that was inside the circle.

The Fall of Jericho (6:8-21)

Joshua commands and the people do as God has bidden. On the seventh day the horns blow, the people shout, and the walls of Jericho fall. God's power is obviously the cause. The people's obedience has been rewarded. Now God commands that the city be utterly destroyed. Only Rahab and her family are saved.

Archeology has shown that Jericho's walls did fall and that the city was burned. However, the date of that destruction does not coincide with the general era of the conquest. Possibly an earlier victory by tribes related to Israel has been incorporated here. That would still, after all, be part of the history of Israel's occupation of Canaan.

Notice that the text does not say that the shouts caused the walls to fall. The people shouted, the horns blew, and the walls fell. It is God's power that has destroyed the fortifications—God's power abetted by the people's detailed obedience.

There are at least two theories about just why the walls

fell. One is that the walls were weak, possibly left unrepaired by a sickly population. Another is that an earthquake might have occurred—the Jordan Valley does run along an unstable fault line. But this is not the author's way of thinking. He is trying to show the unparalleled power of God, not give a scientific explanation of each event.

The *trumpets* are ram's horns, not metal trumpets as we know them.

The reference to *shouting* is another instance of minor story variation. In 6:5 the horn is the signal to shout. In 6:16 the people wait for Joshua's command. In 6:20 there is confusion as to whether shouting or trumpets come first. Obviously this does not change the story's meaning at all. It simply shows that the writer probably had more than one version of the story to work with.

The ban, or *herem,* is when a city and all within it are *devoted to the Lord* and are to be destroyed. The people may take nothing as booty. The city will not be occupied. Everything in it must be destroyed except the precious metals, which must go into the Lord's treasury. This practice incorporates several ideas. One is the complete annihilation of God's foes. No ungodly person or thing should be left to taint Israel. Another is that the victory is presented as a sacrifice to God. The people get no material reward. They recognize that the victory is God's alone. They are risking battle in obedience to God, not for the gain of booty.

Or perhaps the city was afflicted with disease. Snails which serve as intermediate hosts for a parasite that causes schistosomiasis have been found in Jericho. Second Kings 2:19 states that the water in Jericho is bad. This might explain the total destruction, but it does not explain why Rahab and the metal objects were spared. Certainly the author sees the destruction as primarily an act of reverence and obedience. The people must prove their absolute loyalty by resisting the temptation to take articles of value that rightly belong to God. After all, it was God's power that brought the city down.

The writer shows no concern for the people of Jericho. Possibly he has not gone so far as to consider God's love for everyone. Or perhaps he is so intent upon illustrating God's absolute power and the need for absolute obedience that he cannot deal with such a complicated issue.

Rahab Spared (6:22-27)

Joshua keeps faith with the spies' promise to Rahab. Her cooperation with God is rewarded. The city's destruction then proceeds as commanded. The prostitute who hid Joshua's spies now joins the people of Israel. Eventually she will wed Salmon, bear a son, Boaz, and through him become an ancestress of David and of Jesus.

The curse on Jericho is a solemn, permanent thing. Jericho is off limits forever. In 1 Kings 16:34 Hiel of Bethel attempts to rebuild Jericho and reaps the tragedy of the curse.

First Attack on Ai Fails (7:1-26)

Joshua moves on to Ai. He sends out spies, but they are overconfident. The city is on a high ridge and is stronger than the spies suspected. Joshua, believing that God is with him, cannot understand the defeat. Then he learns that there is another reason for that defeat. Someone has sinned by secretly taking booty from Jericho. The man, Achan, is found. He and his family are stoned and burned. The importance of obedience becomes painfully obvious. Another idea also appears, that the act of one member can taint the entire group. Israel is an entity, not a collection of individuals.

Ai means *the ruin*. It is about eleven miles north of Jerusalem. Archaeology has shown that it was a ruin even in Joshua's time. Possibly the story has been confused with the conquest of nearby Bethel, or perhaps an ancient conquest story has attached itself to Joshua's feats. In any case, the writer's point that sin breaks the people's relationship with God stands out clearly.

The name *Achan* is related to the Hebrew word for *trouble*.

Tearing the clothes and putting dirt on the head were signs of grief.

Joshua's anguished attempt to understand his defeat echoes Israel's cries in the wilderness. There they began to lose heart and accused Moses of leading them out of Egypt only to die in the desert (see Exodus 16:3).

A God who allowed the people to suffer defeat would be considered powerless. Joshua wants God to vindicate *your great name* (verse 9) and show God's power.

Sanctify (NRSV) or *consecrate* (NIV) *the people* again points up the concern for ritual purity.

The text does not say so, but it appears that Achan was discovered by using the sacred lots. He took a mantle of Shinar (a cloak from Babylon or made in Babylonian style), about 5.9 pounds of silver, and 1.25 pounds of gold.

The *Valley of Achor* is the Valley of Devastation. This is where the people took Achan to kill him. It is quite a distance from Ai and may be connected to Achan because both the place and the man's name are related to the word *trouble*.

The *heap of stones* (NRSV; NIV = rocks) served as a burial mound, but was also a permanent reminder of the consequences of disobedience. The author returns to his theme of remembering the lessons of history.

Victory at Ai (8:1-35)

Achan's sin has been punished. The relationship between God and Israel has been restored. Now the conquest of Ai can go forward. God promises victory. Joshua obtains that victory by a very clever strategy. He sets up an ambush behind the city. With his main force he draws the Ai soldiers out. He feigns retreat, the hidden force sets fire to the city, then both groups attack the confused enemy. This time God allows Israel to take *livestock* and *plunder* (NIV; NRSV = *booty*) from the doomed city.

Thirty thousand men is quite a large group for an ambush. Quite possibly this is a copyist's error for 3,000 or even thirty.

Verses 3-9 and 10-12 are parallel accounts of Joshua's preparations.

Mount Ebal is a mountain to the north near Shechem. It stands opposite Mount Gerizim. The two form the sides of an important east-west pass. Mount Ebal is quite a distance from Ai, so this story may not belong here in the history. Still, it serves the writer's purpose: to show Joshua's obedience in offering worship and thanks to God as Moses had commanded. As usual, the writer emphasizes the place of the law in the Mount Ebal ceremony. His concern with ritual and liturgical correctness shows also in the care he takes to mention *sacrificed fellowship offerings* (NIV; NRSV = *sacrificed offerings of well-being*) *and burnt offerings,* two specific kinds of sacrifices. Similarly, the writer gives particular details of the altar construction.

Some persons not originally born into Joshua's group *(aliens)* are here incorporated and given full membership privileges.

God must be obeyed and revered completely. No omissions or exceptions should be made, especially where the law is concerned. Therefore there was *not a word which . . . Joshua did not read* (verse 35).

§ § § § § § §

The Message of Joshua 6–8

Obedience—total, complete obedience—that is the key. Achan's disobedience ruined Israel's attack on Ai. Correction of this sinful situation made success possible. The writer never wavers from this basic point: When Israel is obedient, God will bring success. If Israel disobeys, failure will ensue.

We may offer some objections to the writer's simple formula. Life is sometimes more complicated than the writer would make it appear. Still the kernel of truth is there. Sin breaks people's relationship with God. They then have no access to this strength when they need it. There is no substitute for living as God has told us to live.

§ § § § § § §

Joshua 9–12

Introduction to These Chapters

After spectacular successes at Jericho and Ai, Joshua moves on to conquer the rest of God's promised land. Chapters 9 through 12 tell the story of that conquest.

Joshua now faces a more complicated situation. It is no longer a matter of fighting one city at a time. Word of Israel's military feats has spread. Canaanite leaders recognize the grave threat facing them. So, they begin to join together for defense. One group coalesces in the south and one in the north. Joshua will have to deal with both these larger coalitions. In addition one city, acting independently, tries a different strategy, a combination of treachery and diplomacy. This complicates matters slightly, but God helps Joshua through it all to eventual victory.

In these four chapters the writer paints a rather majestic picture of Israel sweeping over Canaan by God's great power. The story is told quickly. The victories are complete. A brief note in chapter 11, however, states that the war took a long time. Naturally, it would. Yet the writer has chosen to compress the action so he can bring out his point, the mighty and irresistible power of God which has given Israel the land of promise.

As in previous chapters, the writer has used several sources. Many of these may be very old and carry excellent historical memories. Some may have become confused over time. This much we know: Israel did overcome the Canaanites and did settle in Palestine, there to remain until 587 B.C.

Here is an outline of Joshua 9–12.
  I. Treaty with the Gibeonites (9:1-27)
 II. Southern Campaigns (10:1-43)
III. Northern Campaigns (11:1-23)
 IV. Conclusion (12:1-24)

Treaty with the Gibeonites (9:1-27)

Joshua has just completed two impressive victories. The Canaanites are becoming alarmed. Some cities are already joining together for mutual defense. One city, however, decides on a different approach. From Gibeon, a group of men set out in ragged clothes, worn-out shoes, and carrying stale food. They come to Joshua in his camp at Gilgal, claiming to be ambassadors from a distant country. The worn shoes and stale food serve as "proof" of the distance they have traveled. They ask for a treaty. Joshua is at first suspicious. His mission is to wipe out the inhabitants of Canaan. What if these men are really Canaanites? Joshua could be going against God's orders. But a treaty with a country far away would not be wrong. Finally he is convinced. He makes the treaty. Then, only three days later, he discovers the trick. Now he is caught between God's original command and the oath he swore by God's name to the Gibeonites. The solution: Do not kill the Gibeonites, but make them slaves. Thus the writer explains the continued presence of Gibeonite slaves in Israelite society.

Here a *king* is the ruler of a single city.

Canaanites on the west side of the Jordan were beginning to form coalitions against Joshua. The territory mentioned covers most of Palestine.

Gibeon was a city six miles northwest of Jerusalem. It was a strong city that had been in league with three other nearby towns.

Hivites were a non-Israelite group living in central Palestine. We know little about the Hivites. In the Old Testament the name is sometimes confused with *Horites,* and sometimes the Hivites of Gibeon are called *Amorites.* So, we cannot be sure just what ethnic group these people belong to.

Verse 14 notes that the Israelites *did not ask direction* (NRSV; NIV = *did not inquire of the Lord*); they failed to ask God's guidance before deciding upon the treaty. Thus they fell into the Gibeonite trap.

The Gibeonites eventually became temple slaves. Verse 23 reflects that later situation for, of course, no temple or house of worship had yet been built. The remark, *the house of my God* reflects, too, the writer's interest in religious places and activities. The story of Gibeonite treachery helps explain why non-Israelites serve in God's house.

Southern Campaigns (10:1-43)

Gibeon was a strong city. The southern kings had apparently counted on Gibeon to help in their fight against Joshua. Instead, Gibeon made peace. Now the southern kings are both frightened and angry. They decide to attack Gibeon, perhaps hoping to force the Gibeonites to join them. But the Gibeonites appeal to Joshua for protection. So Joshua is in the difficult position of having to defend one Canaanite group against another. No matter. He would have had to fight the southern coalition sooner or later anyway.

Despite the mess Joshua has gotten into, God still promises to be with him. Through the night Joshua marches his men the twenty miles to Gibeon. There he takes the southern kings with a surprise dawn raid. The Canaanite forces panic and retreat. As they run, God sends hailstones upon them. Sun and moon even join to aid Joshua. The kings attempt to hide in a cave, but they are found and slaughtered. Joshua then moves through their cities, removing any remaining resistance. Finally he returns to camp at Gilgal.

Jerusalem, Hebron, Jarmuth, Lachish, and *Eglon* are cities of the south. (See map, page 155.) Eglon is also a personal name. There is some question about whether Eglon is here a city or the king of a city (Debir). In Joshua 12:12-13 both Eglon and Debir are listed as cities.

The writer makes a point to note that more men died from God's *hailstones* than from the warriors' blows. He wants to make sure that we realize this is God's victory.

There has been much debate over the event in verse 13, *the sun stood still.* Some have suggested that the poem should read, *Sun, cease from shining*—be dark or cloudy so Joshua might sneak up on his foes more easily or so that his soldiers will not wilt in the heat. This is not generally accepted, however. Meteor showers and an eclipse have also been suggested as the event behind the poem. But these ideas are not too satisfactory either. Best is a recognition that this is a poem, a work that uses symbols to powerful effect. At the time many people worshiped the sun and moon as deities. The poem shows that Israel's God has power far beyond any pagan imaginings. The sun and moon are God's, to use as God wishes. And Israel's victory is God's wish.

The *Book of Jashar* is a collection of ancient songs.

Makkedah is the site of the cave where the kings tried to hide. The location is uncertain, but it was apparently in the area of Gibeon.

Five trees and *large stones* (NRSV; NIV = large rocks) are landmarks that help make the story more vivid and more memorable.

Putting *feet upon the neck* of a conquered enemy is a common sign of victory.

We have just learned that Joshua defeated the five kings and their armies. Now we learn that the cities and their kings must be conquered individually (verses 29-43). This Joshua does with dispatch. It is possible that the survivors needed to be eliminated and that new kings had risen in the cities. However, it is more likely that this is simply a different version of the earlier story.

Notice that the writer does not list Jerusalem as a city that Joshua conquered. He knows that Israel never occupied Jerusalem until David took it.

He left no one remaining (NRSV; NIV = *they left no survivors*) is a phrase repeated throughout to emphasize Joshua's complete obedience to God.

Northern Campaigns (11:1-23)

Kings from northern Palestine have also joined to fend off Israel's advance. Some of this area is a plain. Kings from these cities have chariots and horses, weapons which Israel does not have. Still, God promises victory. An important part of the strategy will be to hamstring the horses and burn the chariots.

Joshua does as he has been told. In a surprise attack he cripples the horses before they can be hitched up, sets fire to the chariots, and routs the assembled army. Then he turns back to overcome their individual cities. This time the Israelites are allowed to take booty, but they must kill all the inhabitants.

Hazor, Madon, Shimron, Achshaph, Naphothdor, and *Mizpah* are cities or territories in the north. (See map, page 155.)

Hazor's king headed the northern confederation, and his is the only city in this area that was burned.

Arabah sometimes refers to the Dead Sea. Here, however, it includes the whole Jordan valley.

Chinneroth (NRSV; NIV = Kinnereth) is the Sea of Galilee.

Merom is probably a creek flowing from the mountains of upper Galilee to the Sea of Galilee.

The writer is emphatic about the total destruction of Israel's foes, saying in verse 11 that there *was no one left who breathed* was not spared (NRSV; NIV = *anything that breathed*).

Although the writer makes the conquest seem swift, the author of this portion recognizes that the fight for Canaan was a difficult one, and took *a long time* (verse 18).

If the Canaanites had given up without a fight, there would have been no need to slaughter them. Yet the writer knows from later history that Canaanite elements remaining within Israel made it easy for the people to turn toward idols. He believes that God does not want Canaanites mixed in with the chosen people. So, he says that God *hardened their hearts* against Israel. Thus, there is an excuse for their total destruction. This may seem odd thinking to us, but the writer has a message to convey about the importance of staying clear of pagan influences, and this is one way he does it.

The *Anakim* are a race of giants. In verse 22, the writer recognizes that some of this group remained in cities on the coast. One of those cities, Gath, later gave the world Goliath.

Conclusion (12:1-24)

This is a summary of Joshua's conquest. It differs at some points from the previous accounts. Possibly this portion comes from a separate source. The chapter includes information about conquests on the west side of the Jordan as well as those on the east. In verses 12 and 13 Eglon and Debir appear as two cities, whereas the earlier accounts listed Debir as king of Eglon.

§ § § § § § §

The Message of Joshua 9–12

Power and gift—if one had to characterize the message of Joshua 9–12 in a few words, these two would do it well. The stories of swift, total conquest show God's tremendous power working at every turn. The miracles, the sudden victorious attacks, and the enemies' panic emphasize God's unlimited force. Gift, while it never appears in the text, is a central point of the stories. The Promised Land has been conquered, not by Joshua's brilliance nor by Israel's strength, but by the power of God. Israel has not earned the land; it is a gift from God. So the meaning is this: The almighty God cares for the people, fights for them, and will give them the gifts that have been promised to them. For their part, they must remember that what they have is not theirs by merit, but as a gift from God. That core message is as valid for us today as it was 2,500 or more years ago.

§ § § § § § §

Introduction to These Chapters

The main battles are over. Joshua and his people have
general control of the Promised Land. Now it is time to
settle down. Chapters 13–21 tell how the twelve tribes, by
lot, obtained their portions. The author gives detailed
listings of cities and boundaries assigned. Chapters 20
and 21 also detail the establishment of two special kinds
of cities. In the land distribution, as in the battles before,
God is the commander and supervisor.

The material in these chapters comes from many
sources. It is even more of a jumble in spots than we have
found in previous chapters. The lists of towns and
boundaries come from various times and appear to have
been updated here and there along the way. So, we
cannot be sure exactly what lands the tribes received at
the actual time of conquest. The lists do give us a general
idea, however. The map on page 155 shows the
approximate area each tribe occupied.

One question has bothered scholars: Did the tribes
really distribute the land by lot as described, or do the
lists merely reflect geographical realities—the places
where each tribe eventually chose to settle? The
boundaries as given probably do reflect some natural
settlement patterns and population shifts over the
centuries. The fact, however, that the text gives us two
accounts of a distribution at two different sites, suggests
that some sort of initial planned distribution did take
place under the leadership of Joshua.

These chapters include another small problem, that of the twelve tribes. Here and in many other Old Testament books, the number twelve is highly significant. Yet we can find differing lists of tribal names. The twelve tribes that receive territories here are: Reuben, Gad, Judah, Benjamin, Simeon, Asher, Dan, Zebulun, Issachar, Naphtali, Manasseh, and Ephraim. But Levi and Joseph were two of Jacob's twelve sons. What about them?

The tribe of Levi is called by God to serve as priests. They have no specific territory but are assigned certain cities throughout Israel. Joseph also receives no allotment. However, two of Joseph's sons, Manasseh and Ephraim, receive shares. The total of territories thus remains at twelve.

These chapters show God's people working together at God's command to form a cohesive nation. The author, writing in exile, was especially concerned with the tribes sticking together. His attention to the details of ancient land holdings, as those details had come down to him, may also reflect his exilic setting. After all, if the people were soon to return home, it might be important to remind everyone just who was supposed to own what. It would also help to maintain hope if people could remember that God had given them this land. The boundaries the writer describes are, of course, ideal ones. Israel very seldom controlled territory that actually matched this description.

These chapters may be outlined as follows.
I. Land Still Unconquered (13:1-7)
II. Inheritance of the Transjordan Tribes (13:8-33)
III. Division Among Remaining Tribes (14:1–19:51)
IV. Special Cities and Conclusion (20:1–21:45)

Land Still Unconquered (13:1-7)

Joshua's sweep of Palestine is over. Israel controls most of the land. Yet some areas remain unconquered.

We know from later history that some of this territory would never be taken, or would be held only briefly. Most of this unconquered land lies in the west near the Mediterranean and in the hills to the north. In Judges, Samuel, Kings, and other books we will find numerous military struggles in these areas. For now, though, God commands that the people distribute and take hold of the land. God promises to drive out before them any remaining foes.

Joshua will be distributing land on the west side of the Jordan to *nine and one-half tribes*—nine tribes plus half of Manasseh. We noted in chapter 1 that two and one-half tribes had already been promised land on the east side of the river.

Inheritance of the Transjordan Tribes (13:8-33)

Here we read of the land east of the Jordan that belonged to Reuben, Gad, and half of Manasseh. The text indicates that Moses had already set these tribes' inheritance. You can see approximately where these tribes settled in the map on page 155.

The east bank tribes failed to drive out the Geshurites and the Maacathites (verse 13). This note may be simply an explanation of these Canaanites' presence within Israel. It may, however, also be a mild rebuke for Israel's not completing the task of clearing out the land.

The tribe of *Levi* is one of priests and religious teachers. Levites served in sanctuaries and later in the Temple, but ranked lower than the priests descended from Aaron. Levitical priests cared for the sanctuary and its equipment, served as musicians, taught and interpreted the law, and helped in the administration of justice. The Levites received no exclusive territory. Instead they were assigned to key cities throughout Israel.

Division Among Remaining Tribes (14:1–19:51)

Here the writer describes the distribution of the land to the west of the Jordan. In chapter 14 the distribution takes place at Gilgal; in chapter 18 it takes place at Shiloh. The two locations suggest that the writer had two versions of the story available to him.

The map on page 155 shows the approximate areas each tribe received. As we mentioned earlier, these ancient boundary lists may have been altered over time. As they stand now, the boundaries recorded in Joshua correspond fairly well with land areas held in the time of David.

Land allotted to three individuals receives special note. The men are Joshua, Caleb, and Othniel. Joshua, having led the people faithfully, receives a city of his choice in the Ephraimite hills. Caleb, Moses' other confident spy, receives the city he spied upon, Hebron. The special attention given to Othniel is a little more complicated. He has taken a city and received Caleb's daughter for his wife as a reward. His land allotment, however, is arid. His wife, therefore, asks her father to provide access to water for them. This Caleb does. The story is important because it explains why a particular group in the Negeb has claim to certain springs.

Notice that, while earlier accounts suggested that Joshua had thoroughly conquered the land, here the tribes must still take their land from some remaining inhabitants. The Anakim, for instance, are still at Hebron. This is yet another instance of multiple traditions.

Before Israel entered the Promised Land, Caleb, along with Joshua and ten others, spied out the land. He was a Kenizzite, a member of a clan of Edom. He was not, therefore, an Israelite by blood. This bit of information seems meant to explain the membership of some foreign elements within Israel. The story of Caleb's inheritance appears twice, in 14:13 and in 15:13.

Othniel is a kinsman, not a full brother, to Joshua. They come from the clan of Kenaz but have different fathers.

The *Negeb* is a very dry area in the south of Palestine.

The tribe of Joseph has been divided into two parts, Ephraim and Manasseh. Half of the Manasseh tribe receives land on the west bank. In 16:9-10 Ephraim has some towns within Manasseh's territory.

Shiloh maintained an important sanctuary for many years. The ark of the covenant remained in Shiloh until it was taken by the Philistines in 1050 B.C.

The total of cities in 15:36 is fifteen, not fourteen.

The list in 19:6 includes fourteen, not thirteen cities.

The tribe of Dan (19:47) lost its original inheritance. It then moved to Leshem (Laish), and changed that city's name to Dan.

Special Cities and Conclusion (20:1–21:45)

God has already commanded that the people set up two special kinds of cities. These are the cities of refuge and the Levitical cities. These cities would play particular roles in establishing and maintaining Israel's national strength.

Cities of refuge were places where a person who had accidentally killed someone could go for safety until a trial could be held. Otherwise a lynch mob of the deceased's relatives would dispatch him immediately.

Levitical cities were the places where Levites would settle. There is some confusion in the Old Testament about whether or not Levites actually owned this land exclusively. Whatever the situation, these cities scattered throughout the land assured that religious workers would be spread across the area.

These two special kinds of cities aided Israel's development greatly, especially in its early years. The cities of refuge helped avoid needless infighting and ongoing vendettas. The Levitical cities made religious teaching and worship widely available. These cities made it easier for the tribes to stick together, to solidify their common family identity, to maintain a constant faith, and to continue sharing a common religious heritage.

Foreigners (aliens), as well as Israelites, could use the cities of refuge. This might easily eliminate some unnecessary foreign wars. It was also a mark of compassion, an important factor in Israel's ethical development.

Hebron is a city of refuge, a Levitical city, and the inheritance of Caleb. The writer tries to explain this complicated situation in 21:11-31 by saying that the fields outside the city were actually Caleb's.

There were forty-eight Levitical cities (21:41), approximately four to each tribe, although division was not exactly equal.

§ § § § § § §

The Message of Joshua 13–21

By following God's commands, Israel was able to establish an orderly, cohesive nation. Fair division of land, plus establishment of Levitical cities and cities of refuge, reduced the probability of internal quarrels. The tribes could live together in peace and, with that internal peace, would gain strength to face external foes. Most important, these institutions that would make the nation strong came from God. God, even now, was still providing for the people.

More generally, the message is that God does want the people to live in peace. God not only wants this, but works to help it happen. God provides institutions and processes that make it easier to get along together. Our part is to obey commands and to use the institutions and rules God has given to develop a good communal life.

§ § § § § § §

Introduction to These Chapters

These chapters mark the end—the end of Israel's
conquest period, the end of Joshua's life, and the end of
the book of Joshua. The largest battles are over. The
tribes from east of the Jordan can go home. The
remaining tribes can move to their assigned territories.
The people can work in peace to build a new nation. And
yet, misunderstanding of one event, the building of an
altar, threatens to undo everything. The matter is settled,
however, and the nation remains intact.

This is obviously a crucial point in Israel's history, a
time for reflection and stock-taking. We find these
attitudes in two farewell addresses given by Joshua. They
wrap up all that Israel's experience and Joshua's own
example have taught throughout the book. In the first
address Joshua pleads with the people to obey God to
they may continue to prosper in God's strength. In the
second he leads the people in a covenant renewal, a
conscious pledge to continue serving God alone. This end
is a new beginning, the start of a new phase of
nationhood. It is a phase to be lived, like past phases, in
faithful obedience.

This section, like the rest of Joshua, has been pieced
together from several sources. Some are probably ancient
remembrances handed down over the centuries. What the
various writers have done with these remembrances
reflects the special concerns of the periods in which those
writers lived. One important period was the time of King

Josiah (640-609 B.C.). A second major period was the Exile (587-538 B.C.). Idolatry, intermingling with Canaanites, and ritual correctness were major concerns from Josiah's time on. The tragic consequences of faithlessness and God's geographically limitless presence were significant ideas during the Exile. Other themes, like national unity and Israel's covenant with God, were important in many periods.

The book climaxes with Joshua's dramatic challenge to covenant renewal at Shechem. This climax is an extremely effective way of placing before readers the book's central point: the importance of obedience and faithfulness.

Here is an outline of these chapters.
I. Departure of the Transjordan Tribes (22:1-34)
II. Farewell Address (23:1-16)
III. Covenant at Shechem (24:1-28)
IV. Three Burials (24:29-33)

Departure of the Transjordan Tribes (22:1-34)

The scene is Shiloh. The main conquest is over. Joshua blesses the tribes of Reuben, Gad, and half of Manasseh as they prepare to cross back over to their homes east of the Jordan. Joshua reminds them to obey the law and to serve God faithfully. Then he sends them off with their share of the collected spoils.

Their departure is not without problems, however. At the Jordan these tribes decide to build an altar. When the other tribes hear of this altar they are incensed. They send representatives to discipline the eastern tribes for what seems to them a terrible religious offense. It nearly comes to war until the eastern tribes explain that they had no intention of making sacrifices there. The altar is to be a memorial and a reminder to all concerned that the eastern tribes are part of Israel, partaking of the same religious beliefs and traditions. God lives on the east as well as on the west bank of the Jordan. This accepted, the tribes again separate in peace.

Why such a fuss over an altar? Early in Israel's history many altars and holy places stood throughout the land. But King Josiah outlawed these holy places. Idolatry had flourished there. Worship should thereafter be controlled by keeping it in Jerusalem. Joshua's people may have feared idolatry among the eastern tribes, but the person most concerned about this altar is really the later writer who had actually seen the proliferation of idolatry in outlying sanctuaries. The conflict and its resolution reflect many of the religious problems Israel had to solve over the centuries, including the questions of worship regulation and the limits or non-limits of God's presence.

Bashan is land east and to the north of the Jordan.

Gilead is another area east of the Jordan.

We do not know the exact spot where the altar was built. It seems, however, to have been on the west side of the Jordan River because one of its functions was to remind the western tribes that their brothers across the river still belonged to Israel. For the writer in exile, this altar incident might have served to remind people that God is God everywhere, not just in the territory of western Palestine.

Peor is a spot located in the Moab area where Israel became involved in idolatry before entering the land of Canaan (see Numbers 25). Note here, as in the story of Achan, that the sins of a few can contaminate the whole nation.

Phinehas is a priest who leads the deputation confronting the eastern tribes. He is the same one who helped settle the problem of idolatry of Peor.

Farewell Address (23:1-16)

This is the first of two addresses Joshua gives. The place is not mentioned. The speech itself is in two parts. Verses 3-10 concentrate on God's promise and its fulfillment. Verses 11-16 are a warning against the temptations of intermarriage and idolatry. Later writers knew all too well the awful consequences of Israel's yielding to such temptations. Joshua's speech is, in fact, a succinct statement of one of the book's basic points: God will be with you just as long as you remain faithful.

Covenant at Shechem (24:1-28)

Joshua's second address comes at Shechem. Here he recounts Israel's history from the call of Abraham through the Exodus to the conquest. He emphasizes that God's power has done all this. Then he challenges the people to put away all other gods. Joshua makes a resounding pledge for himself and his family. The people respond with a similar pledge. Then the tribes leave, each to its own inheritance.

The presence of two farewell addresses suggests two separate traditions, each showing Joshua's concern for Israel's future.

The northern city of Shechem stood between Mount Ebal and Mount Gerizim. It was the site of a long-standing and important shrine.

God sending a *hornet* into battle before Israel may refer to the use of insects as weapons. Since Egypt was sometimes represented as a hornet, the term could also suggest Egypt's weakening of Canaan some years before Israel's entrance. However, the most likely explanation is that the hornet is a symbol of God's great ferocity and power.

The River (verse 14) is the Euphrates. Abraham's family originated in Mesopotamia, where they were pagans.

Joshua warns Israel of possible weakness, saying, *You cannot* (NRSV; NIV = *are not able to*) *serve the* LORD. Perhaps, too, he is using reverse psychology to make the people more determined to remain faithful.

The shrine at Shechem was built around a sacred oak tree.

Three Burials (24:29-33)

The book ends with the notice of three burials: Joshua's, Joseph's, and Eleazar's.

Joshua was buried at the town he had chosen, Timnathserah. A brief eulogy (verse 31) shows Joshua's influence. The writer notes that Israel served God all of Joshua's days and even after his death, so long as any of his contemporaries remained.

Joseph had died much earlier in Egypt. When the people left, they took Joseph's bones with them. They finally buried the bones in Joseph's family tomb at Shechem. (See Genesis 50:25-26.)

Eleazar was the son of Aaron and father of Phinehas (the man who had mediated the quarrel over the altar). Eleazar was buried in Phinehas's town of Gibeah.

§ § § § § § §

The Message of Joshua 22–24

These chapters, especially Joshua's speeches, pound away at a basic Deuteronomic point: God is the power that protects and saves you. If you remain faithful to God you will have success; if you do not, you will reap disaster. Joshua's challenge to the people at Shechem invites all to join in the congregation's affirmation: *we also will serve the* LORD, *for he is our God*.

The warnings about the temptations of idolatry are all too poignant. Israel had, by the time of the earliest Deuteronomic writers, forsaken God and gone after idols. Even when overt idolatry had been controlled, faithlessness continued. Finally, the nation had collapsed. Yet the call was still there. The people could still return to God. They could again affirm with Joshua: . . . *as for me and my household, we will serve the* LORD. The writer hoped that his people would do just that.

As for us, we have the glad and the sad experiences of Israel to learn from. We, too, are tempted to turn from God. But we, like Israel, can also respond to the challenge. We can choose this day, and every day, whom we will serve.

§ § § § § § §

Introduction to Judges

Name

The title refers to this book's main characters, the judges. The Hebrew concept of "judge" differs somewhat, however, from our American use of the word. The biblical persons called judges were tribal or national leaders. Often they were military commanders. Sometimes they settled disputes or offered advice. They gained their leadership positions informally or by popular acclaim. Many judges displayed exceptional wisdom, unusual skill in organization, or personal charisma. These were individuals in whom the people could see God's Spirit at work. It was this divine spirit that gave the judges their talents. Since Israel had no king or other central political figure, the judges played an important role in Israel's survival. They provided administrative and military leadership to a new, loosely organized nation.

Classification

Jews consider this book the second of the "former prophets." And, like the book of Joshua, it does exhibit a prophetic viewpoint. Christians, however, usually call this a historical book because it deals directly with the history of Israel and forms part of the epic historical work that includes most of Deuteronomy through 2 Kings.

Author

Who wrote the book of Judges? That is a complicated question. Scholars believe that the book grew over several centuries. We can recognize at least four major steps in that growth. First came the oral tradition. From the actual time of the judges up to about 950 B.C. people told stories about these leaders, passing the tales on from generation to generation. Between 950 and 800 B.C. someone collected these stories and wrote them down. Around 615 B.C. one or more writers, whom we call the first Deuteronomic historians, included these stories in a great history of Israel. After the destruction of Jerusalem in 587 B.C., another historian of the Deuteronomic school edited a final version.

So, who was the author of this book? Many people were. But the persons who did the most to put the book in the form we have today were the Deuteronomic historians. These were the same ones who prepared and edited the final version of Joshua. For convenience we call them (or him) D. Where possible we also try to distinguish the time period a particular passage comes from.

Style

The style of Judges varies because so many people contributed to it. We find earthiness and a sense of humor mixed with judgmental comments and dry connecting paragraphs. Still, throughout the book we can see one obvious formula repeated over and over, as described in the NRSV. *The Israelites did what was evil in the sight of the* LORD, *and the* LORD *gave them over to . . .* and *the Israelites cried out to the* LORD *and the* LORD *raised* up a *deliverer . . . and the land had rest* or as phrased in the NIV, *the Israelites did evil in the eyes of the* LORD, *and the* LORD *handed them over to . . . and the Israelites cried out to the* LORD *and the* LORD *raised up a deliverer . . . and the land had peace.* With this formula one of the later editors tied his string of stories together and made a theological point all at the same time.

Purpose

The writers' purpose was, of course, to preserve Israel's history. But it was more than that. D and the others wanted to convey the lessons of history, to show the nation what it must do to survive and prosper. These writers wanted to encourage faithfulness and obedience in a people who could easily go astray. They wanted to warn the people of the consequences of disobedience and to remind them that God could be depended upon, no matter what the danger.

The Times

What were the times like? Since the book grew over so many centuries we have to deal with several different times. First is the time of the judges themselves, 1200–1050 B.C. This was just after Joshua's conquest of Palestine and before Israel chose its first king. The time was a very unsettled one. Israel still had to fight to maintain its hold on the land. The nation was only loosely organized. It was surrounded by enemies, all trying to move into or regain land that Israel held. There was Ammon east of the Jordan, there was a Canaanite confederation in north-central Palestine, there were Philistines on the west, Moabites to the southeast, and Midianite nomads who ranged to the east and south of Israel. (See the map "The Ancient Near East," found on page 156.)

Israel was frequently at war with these enemies. Unity among the tribes was essential. But Israel had no king. God was to be their only ruler. So, in times of special need, divinely inspired judges took on specific leadership tasks.

The religious situation under the judges was one of alternating faith and faithlessness. When they were faithful, the people depended upon God for protection and leadership. They recognized God's spirit working through the judges. The tribes periodically met to worship God at central sanctuaries, including Shiloh, Bethel, Gilgal, and Mizpah. Some individuals had home worship centers as well. Nonetheless, this was a primitive time. Faith and worship often went awry. Superstition ran high, and divination was a common practice. Idolatry crept in. Ethics were not the highest. We find many cases of sexual laxity, treachery, thievery, and violence here. Low morality was common and was sometimes approved or taken for granted.

The time of the seventh-century historian was a more organized one. But Israel had fallen into gross idolatry. So, the seventh-century writer's concern focuses on pagan influence and idol worship.

By the time of the exilic editor, Israel's land had been destroyed. The defeated Jews feared that God had rejected them or was powerless to help them. This editor used the stories of the judges to show that an all-powerful God will continue to fight for Israel if the people will only respond in obedience.

Theological Perspective

The main theological points in Judges are the same as those of Joshua. The writer emphasizes God's power, desire to help Israel, and faithfulness in fulfilling promises, and the importance of obedience. If the people will obey, God will defend them and enable them to prosper. If they do not obey, disaster will befall.

Here, as in Joshua, we encounter a problem with violence. These stories frequently show God an advocate of bloodshed. Why should the biblical writers portray God this way? One reason lies in human nature. It is very easy in time of war to assume that God hates the enemy as much as we do. Ancient peoples were no different from ourselves in that respect. They gleefully reported every detail of the foe's defeat and attributed it all to a vengeful God. Second, we must consider that early Israel may not yet have come to recognize God's love for all people. Very old stories tend to think of God's love for Israel. Third, a concern for preserving historical material or a reluctance to get into complex questions of God's character may have led a later, more sophisticated editor to let the ancient stories stand without revision or comment. A fourth possibility is that the writer saw God using the world as it is, not the world as we might wish it to be. In a violent world, God is shown moving in violent events toward long-term goals.

Conclusion

Judges, then, is not a simple book. It is an important one, though. It provides both vital historical information and a religious perspective on God's acts in history. This perspective is one that we need to consider in thinking through our own faith.

Judges 1

Introduction to This Chapter

After the death of Joshua . . .—with his first words the
writer links this book to the preceding one in his series.
We know that the history begun in Joshua is now
continuing in the book of Judges.

Next we find a curious question in verse 1: *Who shall go
up first for us against the Canaanites?* (NRSV; NIV = *Who
will be the first to go up and fight for us against the
Canaanites?*). The book of Joshua has just told us all about
Israel's conquest of Palestine. Why now this question of
who will go first to fight? There are two possibilities.
One is that this is a different version of the basic
conquest, one in which Joshua is not a major hero. The
second possibility is that after Joshua's conquest the land
was still not completely under Israel's control. Joshua
14–18 suggests this kind of situation. These stories, then,
would be the stories of each tribe's efforts to take control
of its territory. Whatever the case, we begin with a
recognition that Israel had to fight for the land. As the
book goes on we realize that Israel must continue to fight
to maintain its possession.

Judges 1–2:5 is a complicated mixture of material. We
find here some duplicates from Joshua and some
passages that differ from the Joshua narrative. One big
difference is that now the tribes are working separately
rather than as a unit. Another is that there is no one
leader. Only a tribe, Judah, is mentioned as leading the
way. We also find some differences in the areas

conquered. The battles may have taken place after Joshua, or the differences may be due to variations in ancient memories.

The purpose of this section is to preserve as much information as possible, to provide a transition from the book of Joshua, and to establish this writer's unique interpretation of Israel's history in this period.

The outline of this section has just two parts:
I. Many a Battle (Judges 1:1-36)
II. Departure from Gilgal (Judges 2:1-5)

Many a Battle (Judges 1:1-36)

This section opens with the notice that Joshua has died. The writer then presents a series of battles which various tribes fight individually or in small groups. He repeats the story of Caleb's daughter, Achsah, and her request for a water source in her husband's arid territory (see Joshua 15:16-19). In verses 22-26 the writer tells a new story, the taking of Bethel. The book of Joshua never mentions Bethel's capture. Now the tribe of Joseph gains access to the town with the help of a traitor.

Verses 27-36 show one of the writer's main concerns quite clearly. These verses repeatedly point out Israel's failure to drive out the Canaanite inhabitants. 1:19 showed Judah unable to drive out the inhabitants of the plain. In contrast, verses 27-36 do not say the tribes *could not*, but they *did not* drive out their enemies. This is a strong rebuke. The writer knew that these Canaanite remnants would eventually lead Israel into idolatry. Such faithlessness would one day bring disaster. So he points the finger, saying, "See, your history of disobedience stretches all the way back to your settlement in this land."

The people did try to follow God's will. They *asked* (NIV; NRSV = *inquired of) the* LORD, probably by using the sacred lots, to determine which tribe should lead out.

Adonibezek was the prince of Bezek (location

uncertain). Since Adonibezek eventually ended up in Jerusalem, it is possible that the name is a misspelling of Adonizedek, king of Jerusalem.

As Adonibezek's remark shows, mutilation (*cut off his thumbs and big toes,* verse 6) was common practice. It not only humiliated the ruler, it made him unfit for battle.

Seventy kings (verse 7) is a large number. Seventy was also a standard size for a council. Adonibezek has taken, in his time, many important prisoners. Now he is reaping his due.

Captives usually ate table scraps (*picked up scraps,* verse 7).

Verse 8 speaks of an attack on Jerusalem. The attack was not totally successful, however. Verse 21 and Joshua 15:63 indicate that neither Benjamin nor Judah could evict the Jebusites from the city. Subsequent history indicates that Israel did not control Jerusalem until David took it.

Caleb was one of the spies who visited Hebron before Israel's entrance into Palestine. Of the twelve spies, only Caleb and Joshua believed that the land could be taken.

Othniel was a kinsman of Caleb. The term *brother* should not be taken literally. Both are from the non-Israelite clan of the Kenizites, but Caleb's father is Jephunneh (Joshua 15:13).

The *Negeb* is an arid area in the south of Palestine.

The *Kenites* were a people friendly to Israel who lived to the south of Palestine. Moses' father-in-law was a Kenite.

Jericho is sometimes called the *City of Palms*.

Gaza is a city on the plain of southwest Palestine. Verse 19 belies the claim of victory in Gaza, indicating that Judah could not drive out its inhabitants. Over the years Israel seldom controlled this area effectively.

Verse 19 refers to chariots with iron parts, not ones made completely of iron.

Land of the Hittites (verse 26) is the remains of an ancient empire in Asia and Syria.

The cities mentioned in verses 27-35 form two east-west chains of fortresses. These fortresses effectively hemmed in Ephraim and Manasseh on the north and south.

The *Amorites* (verses 34-36) are a Canaanite tribe.

Departure from Gilgal (Judges 2:1-5)

An angel now appears to offer Israel direct guidance. He moves Israel's base camp from Gilgal to Bochim. There he delivers a message from God, reminding Israel of God's act of deliverance in the Exodus. He speaks of God's promise to keep the covenant with Israel. Then he warns the people that failure to break away completely from the Canaanites and their religion will bring disaster. Again we recognize the writer's special concern. He knows that this is exactly what did happen.

Gilgal is a city near the Jordan in central Palestine. This was Joshua's main base throughout the conquest.

The location of Bochim is unknown. This city's name means *weepers*. In verse 4 the people weep at the thought of their possible disobedience. The move from Gilgal to Bochim may have poetic value: It parallels Israel's move from a position of obedience and victory to a position of disobedience and weeping.

§ § § § § § §

The Message of Judges 1

These verses are clearly a warning against the temptations of faithlessness and disobedience. The writer insists that God is faithful but that the people have not been faithful to God. They failed to complete the task of conquest God had assigned them. That failure would lead to idolatry and eventual ruin.

This is one variation of the message that the writer emphasizes throughout his history. Our success comes in obedience; our failure comes in disobedience. We today may recognize that all disaster is not necessarily the result of faithlessness. Yet, much of our misery, whether personal, national, or global, stems from someone's failure to live as God has intended. Perhaps we, like Israel, need to recognize the danger of our ways—and weep.

§ § § § § § §

Judges 2

Introduction to These Chapters

Another introduction—that's what we find in Judges 2:6–3:6. In the preceding section the writer had introduced us to the book of Judges. He had made a clear transition from the book of Joshua. He had told us of Joshua's death. Now here we find Joshua again. It looks like Judges 2:6–3:6 was the opening of an earlier version of the book. The final editor kept what he had and added an introduction of his own (1:1–2:5) before it.

The 2:6–3:6 introduction has two parts. Verses 6-10 form a connecting link to the book of Joshua by reviewing Joshua's death and burial. The accounts of this hero's tribal dismissal and death echo Joshua 24:28-31. In 2:11–3:6 someone has written a summary of what we will find in the book of Judges. It is a story of faithlessness and disaster, yet an affirmation of God's desire to save Israel if only the people will turn to God. This writer explains the role of the judges and how God used them to help Israel. The section concludes with two lists of non-Israelite peoples whose continued presence in Palestine contributed to Israel's downfall.

The material in these chapters obviously comes from several sources. We find numerous repetitions and variations. The writer apparently wanted to save every tradition, and did so despite the inconsistencies this created.

Within this material we find some important theological concepts. The writer outlines for us a pattern of events that will recur throughout the book. He sees the period of the judges as a repeating cycle of defection, oppression, prayer, and deliverance. Here and throughout the book he uses a set formula to begin a story, as seen in verse 11: *And the Israelites did what was evil in the sight of the* LORD (NRSV; NIV = *the Israelites did evil in the eyes of the* LORD). The main point of the writer's whole historical epic comes through clearly in Judges: If the people obey God, they will prosper; if not, they will suffer. The writer (or several writers) also tries in these chapters to explain a theological puzzle, the problem of why God ever allowed these alien peoples to remain in the land when their presence caused so much trouble. In Joshua the answer was that Israel itself failed to rout the inhabitants. Israel thereby disobeyed God's command and suffered accordingly. In Judges 2:20-22 and 3:1-6 the writer provides additional explanations for the disastrous situation.

Here is an outline of this brief, but complex, section of Judges:
  I. Joshua Dies (2:6-10)
  II. Israel's Infidelity (2:11-23)
  III. Israel Among the Nations (3:1-6)

Joshua Dies (2:6-10)

Joshua commands the tribes to go out from their common camp to settle in their allotted lands. Then Joshua dies, as does his whole generation. This passage is similar to, but does not have exactly the same wording as Joshua 24:28-31. Possibly that passage once ended the book of Joshua while this one began the book of Judges.

Judges 2:7 and 2:10 work together to set the scene for the rest of the book. The writer notes that the elders who had seen God's mighty works in the conquest remained faithful, but . . . another generation grew up who did not know the LORD (verse 10). That's what this book is about—the faithlessness of succeeding generations and God's efforts to deal with them.

Timnathheres is a variant spelling of Timnathsereh. The *h* and *s* have been exchanged. Both spellings refer to the town Joshua inherited. Timnathsereh, used in the book of Joshua, means *left-over portion*. Timnathheres, used here, means *portion of the sun*. The second version would be a little more flattering to Joshua, but it may be nothing more than a copying error.

Israel's Infidelity (2:11-23)

Verses 11-20 give us an outline for the book to follow. Over and over we will see the same sequence played out: The people forsake the Lord and go after Canaanite gods. God becomes angry and refuses to protect Israel. The people suffer. Then God pities them and gives them a leader or judge who saves them. Yet when the crisis has passed, the people again turn away.

In verses 20-22 the writer offers two reasons why God does not drive out all the Canaanites from the land. The first is that the people have already turned faithless. They have broken their covenant with God. God is no longer bound to protect them and, in anger, God refuses to remove the elements which are destined to bring Israel to ruin. The second explanation is that God wishes to test the people, perhaps setting up a kind of trial by fire which God hopes will strengthen and prove the people's loyalty. This second explanation makes God seem less of a punisher and more of a teacher.

In verse 23 we find ourselves back with Joshua again, remembering that God did not give Joshua complete victory over his foes.

One question might bear brief exploration here: Why should people to whom God has been so good turn so readily to Canaanite gods? There are several reasons. All of them together made idolatry an easy step for many Israelites.

The first is intermarriage. With so many Canaanites around, such mixing was bound to take place. Once married, the Israelite could easily be drawn to the spouse's religion, if only to keep family peace.

Another reason for defection was familiarity. They saw the neighbors worshiping these gods, and they thought, why not? In addition, many Israelites may have remembered that their own ancestors worshiped just such idols as these.

A third temptation lay in the gods themselves. These were gods that offered what people desperately wanted: fertility of land and family, success in war, prosperity, and continued life. Such gods would be very attractive.

Not to be discounted, of course, is the nature of some Canaanite worship. These were fertility gods. They were worshiped by acts of sacred prostitution. Obviously this would be appealing.

According to God, the Israelites did evil by serving the Baals. *Baal* is a Canaanite god. The term is usually plural because many worship centers, each with its own idol, flourished throughout Palestine.

Ashtaroth (NIV) is the plural form of Astarte (NRSV), the Canaanite fertility goddess.

In ancient Hebrew thought everything, good and evil, came directly from God. When God was angry God punished Israel by working against the people (. . . *hand of the* LORD *was against them* . . . , verse 15).

The people *prostituted themselves to other gods* (NIV) or they *lusted after other gods* (NRSV). Israel has been unfaithful to God; she has gone after other gods. The image is especially appropriate considering the nature of Canaanite religion.

Israel Among the Nations (3:1-6)

Here the writer attempts to list the peoples who remained within Israel and caused so much trouble. He has used at least two sources which do not agree. In verse 3 there are four nations: the Philistines, the

Canaanites, the Sidonians, and the Hivites. In verse 5 there are six groups: the Canaanites, the Hittites, the Amorites, the Perizzites, the Hivites, and the Jebusites.

Here again the writer tries to explain why God allowed these groups to remain. He offers two reasons: to test the people and to teach war. We have seen the testing explanation before, in verse 22. Teaching war may seem a little strange, but it can have two meanings: (1) to teach the people a painful lesson in obedience through the suffering of war, and (2) to let a new generation of people experience firsthand God's saving power in a major wartime crisis.

§ § § § § § §

The Message of Judges 2

This short passage carries several messages from several hands. The first and most prominent is the story of the later generations' infidelity and the suffering it caused. The second is God's effort to help. The third includes the explanations of why God allowed corrupting alien influences to remain within Israel: to punish, to test, to teach, or to bring the people back.

These verses speak of our frailty and of the weakness of second-hand religion. We, like the ancient Israelites, live among unbelievers. Our neighbors have values and practices that differ drastically from the biblical ideal. It is easy for us to accept their ways. It is easy to ignore God's commands. In the midst of these temptations, we need help. Unfortunately, it may take some suffering to make us realize that we need firsthand experience of God's power in our lives. That experience is one that we can only get through repentance and obedience.

§ § § § § § §

Judges 3

Introduction to This Chapter

Israel had established itself in Palestine. Still, the nations on every side continually pressed. Some wanted to recover territory Israel had wrested from them. All wanted to extend their holdings as far as they could. So Israel's claim to the land was often threatened. Power shifted from time to time and place to place. Sometimes Israel held its own; sometimes it didn't. The Deuteronomic writers set out to explain these changing fortunes from their own unique theological perspective. These events were not just political or military affairs; they were reflections of Israel's relationship with God.

With Judges 3:7-31 we begin the actual stories of the judges. These verses contain three ancient stories of men who saved Israel from encroaching enemies. None of the men is especially well-known today. Other biblical heroes have overshadowed them in the popular mind. This is due, at least in part, to the fact that these accounts are so short. The first is brief and tells only the basic facts plus their interpretation. The third is just one verse long. Only the second carries enough detail to really be a story.

The first and second stories follow the writer's characteristic formula. They begin with the people of Israel doing evil according to God. They worship idols. The Lord becomes angry and sells them into servitude. When the people cry to God for help, a deliverer is provided. The third story, being only a single verse, lacks the full formula. Yet, packed in among the others, it seems to follow the pattern.

Inclusion of these brief accounts shows the writer's determination to preserve all the historical material available. The repeated formula shows his concern to interpret the stories in theological terms.

The writer uses these and subsequent stories to show how Israel is supposed to relate to God. Here we begin a book-long series of examples where faithlessness breeds disaster while return to God brings salvation and peace. God is Israel's king and commander. Trust and obedience to this divine king is Israel's key to survival and success.

Here is an outline of these three accounts:
  I. Othniel (3:7-11)
 II. Ehud (3:12-30)
III. Shamgar (3:31)

Othniel (3:7-11)

In this first story the enemy who overcomes Israel is Cushanrishathaim. His center of power is not known. When the people cry to God for help, God sends Othniel as deliverer. This is the same Othniel who appears in Judges 1:12-15, the kinsman of Caleb who conquered Debir and married Caleb's daughter. Othniel is a Kenizite, that is, an Edomite. His clan has, however, been incorporated into the Israelite tribe of Judah. Of all the judges he is the only one from the south.

Verse 10 shows well the characteristics of a judge: the spirit of the Lord was upon him, he judged Israel, he went to war, and with God's help he overcame the enemy.

Cushanrishathaim means *double wickedness*. Verse 8 identifies him as king of Mesopotamia. The reference is rather vague. Possibly he ruled an area in northern Mesopotamia. Translation difficulties and historical factors make it hard to pinpoint his realm, however. Some commentators place Cushanrishathaim as a king of the southern hills. Wherever this conqueror came from, Othniel evicted him.

Ehud (3:12-30)

This is a much more detailed story than the other two in this section. Here we find many concrete facts and images. We can picture the events well—perhaps too well. This is a graphic presentation of an extremely gory event. The style, however, serves as indication of a very old story, told and retold, probably with some relish, by generations of rather primitive people.

The enemy now is Eglon, king of Moab. Moab is to the south. Eglon is, however, in league with the Ammonites and Amalekites. The Ammonites inhabit the central area east of the Jordan. The Amalekites are nomads who roam the territory generally. This confederation has moved westward into Jericho. The Israelites in the area must pay tribute. One might liken it to a combination tax and "protection" money.

Finally the people call to God, and God chooses Ehud to save them. Ehud is a characteristic early hero. He wins as much by treachery and wit as by strength. When he goes to deliver the tribute, Ehud carries a concealed sword or dagger. He hands over the money, then he and his company head toward home. Shortly, however, Ehud doubles back to Moab alone. He approaches Eglon claiming to have a special message for him from God. The message is Eglon's death. Ehud cleverly locks the door and escapes while the servants wait outside. Then Ehud marshalls troops from Ephraim and drives the surprised and kingless Moabite army back across the Jordan.

The *Amalekites* may have provided several of the Canaanite tribes with a kind of communications network. Moving around the territory as they did, they could carry messages from one tribe to another, making it easier for these enemies to gang up on Israel.

The *city of Palms* is Jericho.

Ehud was left-handed, probably because of a defect in his right hand. Ironically he was a Benjaminite, and Benjamin was the "son of the right hand." Left-handedness was considered quite unusual, but in Ehud's case it gave him a distinct advantage. Eglon would naturally be somewhat suspicious of even a lone visitor from Israel. He would be watching the right hand for signs of movement. When Ehud's left hand stirred, Eglon was caught off guard. Ehud killed him before he had a chance to defend himself. This is a good example of the Israelite underdog using a handicap to overcome a strong oppressor. Israel, being a small, weak nation, appreciated such stories immensely.

A *cubit* (NRSV) is about 18 inches (NIV).

In verse 19, *the idols* (NIV) or *sculptured stones* (NRSV) cannot be further identified. They may, however, be related to the stones Joshua took from the Jordan and set up in Gilgal (Joshua 4:20).

This story does not specifically say that God's spirit rested upon Ehud as upon the other judges. However, the idea of a *message from God* indicates that Ehud saw himself as God's agent.

Just what room the *roof chamber* (NRSV; NIV = *upper room*) may have been is not clear. The King James Version calls it a *porch*. It may have had two doors, one of which led to an outside balcony. If so, Ehud would have locked both doors and jumped to safety from the balcony. Or, Ehud may have locked a single door and escaped through a room inside the house while the servants were occupied elsewhere.

The location of *Seirah* is not known.

The quick marshalling of an army (*and the Israelites went down*, verse 27) shows Ehud's strong leadership qualities. The people saw him as God's deliverer and willingly followed him.

Shamgar (3:31)

This one verse is probably all the writer knew about Shamgar. The enemy now is the Philistines, who live to the west. The writer reports Shamgar as killing 600 Philistines single-handedly. Presumably this is an exaggeration, one which primitive people might enjoy very much. Whatever the actual facts, Shamgar was able to rid Israel of this Philistine menace.

Shamgar is probably a Hurrian name, suggesting that this hero may not have been a native Israelite at all.

Being the *son of Anath* may mean that Shamgar lived in Beth-Anath in Galilee (a Canaanite city) or that he was a member of a seminomadic tribe (the Hanaans) who sometimes provided mercenaries in the area. If Shamgar was a non-Israelite this would be one of many Old Testament examples of God's using foreigners to save the chosen people.

An *oxgoad* was a metal-tipped instrument used to prod oxen.

§ § § § § § §

The Message of Judges 3

This is a message of history. God has saved the people many times. No matter how often they sin and suffer, when they turn to God they will be saved. People of the Exile knew suffering. The writer offers them the evidence of history to show that there is hope. No matter what Israel's sins (and they have been serious), God can still raise up a deliverer.

The United States has not suffered invasion since its early days. Still, our country could one day fall either from external conquest or from internal weakness. The message of Judges is that there is hope for a nation, even a nation in deep trouble, if that nation will turn to the Lord.

For individuals, too, the message holds. No matter what the sin or the suffering, God can help, if we will only ask for help.

§ § § § § § §

Judges 4–5

Introduction to These Chapters

Content

These chapters tell the story of two judges, Deborah
and Barak. Deborah is the leader and organizer; Barak is
the military commander who carries out Israel's battle for
freedom.

The place is Israel's northern territory. There enemies
are confining Israel to the hills and denying access to the
more prosperous plain areas.

The time is the twelfth century B.C., probably around
1125. Archaeologists have discovered that Taanach,
which figures prominently in the story, was destroyed
about that time.

The enemy is a coalition of Canaanite kings or of
Canaanites and Sea Peoples. These kings have strong
armies with horses, iron chariots, and plenty of weapons.
Israel is militarily weak and does not even know yet how
to work with iron.

The problem, on the surface, is the oppression of these
Canaanites. The people of Israel live in fear, shrinking
back into the hills to avoid confrontation with the
aggressive foe. Back roads are unsafe, caravans are
unable to travel into Israel, farmers can scarcely work
their land. But the underlying problem, as always in
Judges, is Israel's faithlessness to God. Idolatry again
has raised its ugly head, and Israel is suffering because
of it.

The solution comes when the people finally call to God

for help. God does respond by sending help, through Deborah and Barak. These two persons rouse the oppressed people to action. They call upon all the tribes of Israel to form an army. Some, but significantly not all, of the tribes respond. The day of battle comes. The weak, untrained tribesmen face their enemy. Then God, by storm and flood, destroys that enemy, giving Israel freedom and peace.

Structure

These chapters contain two versions of the same story. Chapter 4 is a prose account. Chapter 5 is a poem. That poem is one of the oldest pieces of Hebrew literature we have. It may well have been composed at the time of the event. The prose version of chapter 4 may be a combination of two battle stories, one about a victory over Jabin and one about a victory over Sisera.

The two chapters tell essentially the same story, but they disagree on a few details. In chapter 4 Jabin is king of Canaan, and Sisera is his general. Chapter 5 does not mention Jabin at all. Instead, we find the *kings* of Canaan, who are led by Sisera. Jabin appears in Joshua 11 as king of Hazor. His mention at this earlier time is one reason for suspecting that he does not quite fit into the Deborah story. His absence from chapter 5 supports that suspicion.

A second difference in detail is the scene of battle. In chapter 4 the battle is at the foot of Mount Tabor. In chapter 5 the battle is at Taanach.

A third difference between the two accounts concerns who fought the battle. Chapter 4 mentions only the tribes of Zebulun and Naphtali. Chapter 5, however, gives these two special credit but indicates that other tribes also helped.

Despite these minor differences, each version makes the same point: God, through Deborah and Barak, saves Israel.

Purpose

The writer's general purpose in including these chapters was to preserve Israel's history and to inspire courage and faith, especially in times of oppression. The poem in chapter 5, however, originally had some additional purposes. In the days before writing was common, it served as a teaching tool. It may also have served as a form of popular entertainment. But its most important function was probably to arouse enthusiasm and encourage action when Israelite armies again gathered to face a common enemy. This thrilling story of courage and victory would motivate the assembled recruits to bravery in the coming battle.

Style

Both these versions provide detailed, colorful accounts of events. Both are good examples of storytelling art, though perhaps the poem is a bit more dramatic. The writers build suspense, help listeners identify with Israel's cause and its heroes, and teach well their main points: the power and trustworthiness of God, the need for courage and faith, and the importance of cooperation.

A Moral Problem

In both these pieces, modern readers may find a common Old Testament problem. These stories reveal, even applaud, bloodthirstiness, vengefulness, and deceit. Jael is praised for her treachery and murder "in a good cause." Chapter 5 glories in the misery Sisera's mother experiences as she waits in vain for her son's return. These attitudes are foreign to us and must be recognized as such. Even God's chosen people did not fully understand God in those early days, nor perhaps do we yet.

Outline

Here is an outline of these chapters.

I. The Oppression (4:1-3)

The Oppression (4:1-3)

As is usual in Judges, the writer begins with the formula *And the Israelites again did what was evil in the sight of the LORD* (NRSV; NIV = *the Israelites once again did evil in the eyes of the LORD*). That evil brings oppression upon Israel. Finally they cry for help. The writer connects this story to the major story of chapter 3 by noting that the former hero, Ehud, had died. Chapter 4 skips over Shamgar (Judges 3:31), but the version in chapter 5 does mention him.

Jabin was a Canaanite king from Hazor, in the north. Joshua 11 tells us that Joshua killed Jabin before this story's opening.

Sisera was possibly one of the Sea Peoples. Chapter 5 shows him as a king in his own right, not as Jabin's general. His territory, Harosheth-ha-goiim, was probably near Megiddo, far from Hazor. Nevertheless, this somewhat confused account of the enemy may still indicate that Deborah and Barak faced some kind of confederation of Canaanites and Sea Peoples.

Deborah and Barak Plan (4:4-9)

Out of oppression the people have called. God has heard, and provides two leaders. The chief is Deborah, a prophetess. At God's direction she works with Barak to gather support from the tribes. They assemble an army. Barak insists that Deborah go with the army to battle. Barak knows that the spirit of God is with Deborah. For him, her presence assures the presence of God. Her presence would also make an on-site divine guidance available. Deborah, in an almost teasing way, responds with an ironic prophecy. She tells Barak that he will not gain any great glory in this battle. The victory will come through a woman. First-time hearers of the story, and perhaps Deborah herself, would assume that Deborah is the woman. We learn later, of course, that the heroic woman is actually Jael. This is certainly excellent storytelling technique, but it may also be meant to suggest that a prophet like Deborah can speak with wisdom well beyond his or her own understanding.

Lappidoth is Deborah's husband. He is mentioned only here, so we know nothing about him except his name, which means *torch*.

Barak was apparently a leader from Kedesh. His name means *lightning*. Because of the similarity between "lightning" and "torch" some commentators suggest that Barak and Lappidoth may be the same man. This is possible, but with no more substantial evidence we cannot jump to such an identification.

The Palm of Deborah: Deborah had been acting as a judge, helping people solve problems and discerning God's will, for some time. She apparently had a wide reputation and had a special place where she could be contacted.

Kedesh was a town to the north near the Sea of Galilee.

The Victory (4:10-24)

The troops gather at Kedesh, then go to Mount Tabor. There they await the enemy. It is a strategic position for Israel: Sisera cannot go up into the hills with his chariots, but from the heights Israel can swoop down upon him. Deborah gives the battle cry. The Lord routs the enemy. The writer offers few details here, just the bare bones of events.

Sisera flees, leaving his troops to Barak's destruction. The cowardly general finally seeks refuge in the tent of Heber, the Kenite. Heber's wife, Jael, deceives him with seeming welcome, then kills him brutally and efficiently.

The storyteller approves of Jael's action. We may find it repugnant, but people of that early time did not. A more important point is that Jael risked her own safety to help the people of God. For that she is praised.

The Kenites were nomads. They had allied themselves with the Canaanites, so Sisera had reason to assume he would be safe with them. Jael, however, had her own loyalties, and they lay with the God of Israel.

Barak originally gathered his troops at Kedesh in Naphtali near the Sea of Galilee. Here Heber's tent is near Kedesh by the oak of Zaanannim. It seems strange, though not impossible, that Sisera would flee into a major Israelite stronghold. Some suggest that there were two Kedeshes. If so, Heber would be living near a town to the north of Naphtali's territory.

Kishon is a two-forked stream running from the hills to the Mediterranean Sea. One fork comes from the Mount Tabor area; the other passes by Megiddo and Tanaach.

Sisera asks for water, but Jael gives him goat's milk instead. She may have had a purpose: Some goats' milk has a tranquilizing effect which she could use to dope her victim.

It would be very difficult to drive a tent peg through someone's skull. However, you could kill a sleeping man by driving the peg through the upper neck behind the lower jaw or at the back of the head at the spinal cord.

The Song of Deborah (5:1-31)

This is one of the oldest pieces of literature in the Old Testament. It is a poem, and contains a good deal of imagery plus many repetitions and parallel constructions designed for artistic effect. The writer has surrounded the poem with a little prose frame consisting of verse 1 and the last line of verse 31.

Who composed this song? Verse 1 suggests that Deborah and Barak did. However, by verse 7 the poet is speaking to Deborah, so she cannot be the speaker. It is, of course, likely that Deborah and Barak did give some kind of victory speech after the battle. And it is possible that a portion of their words is preserved in verse 2. The rest of the poem could have been composed by an anonymous poet to fully celebrate the great deeds done through these judges.

After a call for everyone's attention (including the attention of even the greatest), the poem begins. It reminds listeners first of God's power and mighty saving acts in the Exodus and the conquest. Then it goes on to recount the story of Deborah and Barak. The story is similar to that told in chapter 4, but does contain a few variations. (See Structure section in the introduction.)

One variation is in the space devoted to the tribes that fought. In chapter 4 only Naphtali and Zebulun appear. Here each tribe, except Judah, is listed and judged a s to whether or not it contributed to the common good. Those who helped receive praise; those who did not receive censure. This section shows the deep need for cooperation among the loosely organized tribes. It also shows that that cooperation was not always there. It is perhaps natural that those tribes who gave the most lived in the oppressed area, while those who helped least lived farther away.

As in the previous version, the writer is careful to note that Israel fought, but God won the battle. Here we see God using the forces of nature—power of the stars, rain, a flood—to enmire Sisera's chariots and defeat him.

The poet punctuates the story of Sisera's assassination with the picture of his mother's hopeless wait. The writer seems to take pleasure in her agony. Again our ancient Hebrews are not charitable. Yet gloating over an enemy's suffering may be understandable among a people regularly threatened by brutal oppression.

Seir is the chief mountain range of Edom.

The poet depicts God's power by picturing him as a colossus whose marching footsteps shake the earth and whose might disturbs all nature (*the earth trembled* (NRSV; NIV = *shook,* verse 4).

Shamgar is a judge mentioned briefly in Judges 3:31.

Verses 6-7 mention the unsafe conditions in Northern Israel for travelers and even for the settled villagers before Deborah arose.

Verse 8 indicates that Israel was very short on weapons.

Deborah's method of arousing fervor for battle was a common one: Sing the old victory songs.

Machir (makir) is western Manasseh.

Unlike the prose version, we find here no mention of Jabin. The poem has as enemies only an anonymous group of Canaanite kings led by Sisera.

The *Kishon* is a two-forked stream flowing to the Mediterranean. In this version the battle takes place on the fork that flows by Taanach and Megiddo. This is south of chapter 4's Mount Tabor locale.

Meroz is an unknown place or group.

§ § § § § § §

The Message of Judges 4–5

This passage carries the usual Deuteronomic message that God is powerful and will save if Israel will trust and obey. It also emphasizes two additional, though not unique, messages: (1) the importance of cooperation among God's people, and (2) the praiseworthiness of courage in carrying out God's will.

We, like the people of ancient Israel, need to rely on God's power if we are to succeed. On the other hand, we must recognize that courageous action on our part may be needed to implement God's plan for helping us.

§ § § § § § §

Judges 6–8

Introduction to These Chapters

These are the stories of Gideon. Like many other Israelite judges, Gideon is a great military leader. But in other ways he is a different kind of judge. He does not exemplify the faithful, courageous servant of God. He comes from a Baal-worshiping family and town, he is reluctant to accept God's call, he questions God's concern, and he is slow to believe God's promises. Later he proves headstrong, overly aggressive, and self-serving. He recognizes that God alone must be king, yet sets himself up as a formal leader. His work does save Israel, but others of his actions set Isreal up for further disaster. As a judge Gideon is not an unqualified success.

Time

Archaeological findings place Gideon about fifty years before Deborah, that is, around 1175 B.C. The final editor may have been unaware that the stories were out of order. Some commentators, however, see an alternating pattern of good and not-so-good judges within the book as a whole. This could explain Gideon's appearance after Deborah.

Many of these stories show signs of great antiquity. Though they have been passed down and edited over generations, some of the materials may carry surprisingly accurate reflections of the conditions and events they describe.

Place

These stories center in the territory of Manasseh in northern Palestine.

The Enemy

The enemy in these stories is Midian, a nomadic tribe based east of the Jordan. Allied with Midian are Amalekite nomads and possibly others.

Structure

This is a series of stories joined together to form a continuous narrative. There are at least two strands of traditions here. The strands are so thoroughly mingled, however, that one cannot untangle them with any certainty; they may account for the varying descriptions we find of Gideon's character. At one time he is timid, at another extremely aggressive. Sometimes he is faithful and obedient to God; at other times he questions or ignores God. Some of the early stories are very hero-oriented. Other stories emphasize God's action, with Gideon as God's instrument.

Apparently all the storytellers did not hold the same picture of Gideon, nor did they have the same point to make. The final editor has taken care to use the stories to show the importance of recognizing God's kingship and saving power.

Here is an outline of these chapters.
  I. Problems with the Midianites (6:1-6)
 II. Gideon's Call (6:7-32)
III. Invasion and Uncertainty (6:33-40)
 IV. Preparations (7:1-15)
  V. Attack and Victory (7:16–8:21)
 VI. The Story Ends (8:22-35)

Problems with the Midianites (6:1-6)

The story begins with the usual Deuteronomic formula: Israel has done evil, and that evil has brought oppression upon the people. A nomadic enemy has been making swift and frequent attacks, destroying crops and livestock so that Israel faces a severe food shortage. This enemy has a new and awesome weapon: the camel. The people of Israel are so powerless and so frightened that they hide in caves. Finally in their distress they turn to the God whom they had ignored.

The *Midianites* were a nomadic people living east of the Jordan and well to the south. They were perhaps better organized than most nomads, as they had kings. With Amalekites and similar tribes, the Midianites frequently raided Israel.

The *Amalekites* were a nomadic group that ranged over much of Palestine.

People of the East (NRSV; NIV = *eastern peoples*) are miscellaneous tribes from east of the Jordan.

Gaza is a city in southern Palestine near the Mediterranean Sea. The Midianites apparently terrorized all of Palestine at this time.

Gideon's Call (6:7-32)

This section contains two stories: (1) Gideon's encounter with the angel, and (2) Gideon's call to destroy the Baal altar. In the first story God speaks mainly through a messenger. At the end of that story, however, and throughout the next story, God speaks directly to Gideon. The author may have used this device to emphasize Gideon's original distance from God and his growing ability to hear God's voice.

When the angel tells Gideon that God wants him to lead Israel out of oppression, Gideon's response is not one of great faith. First he questions that God even cares for Israel, then he argues that God's plan is senseless, since he and his clan are relatively weak. This is, of course, one reason God has chosen Gideon. Victory from such weakness will make it very clear that the conquering power if actually God's.

The presence of a Baal altar in Gideon's family indicates how pervasive idolatry has become. Family and neighbors alike have turned to Baal. There is no indication that Gideon has previously objected to this.

The name *Gideon* means *hacker*.

Ophrah, Gideon's home, was a town somewhere in Manasseh. Its exact location is unknown. Another Ophrah is in Benjamin.

The oak may have been a place where Baal oracles were given. The angel, however, takes it over for his own purposes.

Gideon has to thresh his wheat at night in a hidden wine press to avoid having it stolen.

An *ephah* is a measure frequently taken as two-thirds of a bushel or more. This would make a lot of bread! It is possible, however, that the ephah varied widely over the centuries and some smaller amount is meant.

Gideon, still not sure about this message, asks God for a sign.

Miraculous burning of the sacrificial food finally convinces Gideon of God's presence.

The *Asherah* pole (NIV; NRSV = *sacred pole*) probably signifies a cult object or objects used in the worship of a Semitic goddess.

In verse 27, Gideon acts during the night rather than the day. Perhaps Gideon hopes no one will know who has vandalized the altar.

Joash defends his son by questioning Baal's power. Apparently his loyalty to Baal is not strong.

Jerubaal means *hacker of Baal* or *Let Baal bring suit*. The writer suggests that Gideon's alternate name came from his altar destruction. However, it is possible that Jerubaal was Gideon's original name. The ending could indicate a person whose god was Baal. The writer would want to explain why one of God's chosen judges should have such a name. This story would give him such an explanation.

Invasion and Uncertainty (6:33-40)

Another Midianite attack! This time they are taking over the Valley of Jezreel, a very fruitful area in the north. Gideon calls men from his own clan and tribe, then sends out an appeal to Asher, Zebulun, and Naphtali. As we shall see, this is more than God had in mind.

Gideon still has doubts, however. He asks God for yet another sign, using a fleece. A fleece placed on a warm rock at evening could generate considerable condensation, even though there was little dew elsewhere. So, the first test does not satisfy Gideon. He tries again. To keep the fleece dry while all around is wet would indeed be a miracle. God, of course, is able to provide such a miracle.

Preparations (7:1-15)

This section contains two more stories. The first is the testing and reduction of Gideon's army. Gideon has massed a huge force. But God wants no doubt left as to whose power won the victory. Gideon must win with only a few men and the might of God.

The second story again shows Gideon's uncertainty. Overhearing a Midianite soldier's account of a dream reassures him, however.

Harod's spring is a spot just south of the Midianite camp.

Moreh is a hill across the valley from Mount Gilboa.

God sifts the soldiers by two tests: outright acknowledgement of fear and the drinking test. Those who knelt down to drink were vulnerable to attack because they weren't watching for the enemy. The others lifted the water in their hands and lapped it. They could still see who was coming. Fearless and alert men would certainly make preferable soldiers.

Jars may be *provisions* instead. However, jars or jugs figure prominently in the upcoming battle.

Barley bread is the symbol for the Israelite farmers in the soldier's dream.

Attack and Victory (7:16–8:21)

This will be God's victory, not Gideon's. The main battle, in fact, will not be won by military strength at all, but by a God-directed trick. Moving at night, Israel simulates a three-sided attack. The surprise alone routs the Midianites. Neither Gideon nor the soldiers can say that their strength overcame the foe.

The remaining parts of the story show Gideon as a military hero pursuing and defeating the Midianites. God figures very little in these stories. Such a contrast with the previous one suggests a different storyteller.

After the initial rout, Gideon calls other tribes to help wipe out the retreating Midianites. The tribe of Ephraim, however, is displeased because it did not get to participate in the battle. Perhaps this is a matter of honor, perhaps a matter of shares in the spoil. Anyway, Gideon mollifies the group.

Next Gideon goes far beyond his original assignment. He chases his foe across the Jordan. There he approaches two cities of his own tribe, but they refuse to aid him. They live too close to the Midianites' home base to risk the foe's displeasure. Again we see the lack of cooperation so common in this period. Gideon punishes these cities. Then he slaughters the two Midianite kings he has captured. Only now do we learn his real reason for pursuing them: They killed his brothers. The saving of Israel has turned into a matter of personal revenge.

Night guard duty is divided into three parts. The *middle watch* is the time during the middle of the night.

Zererah is probably Zarethan in the Jordan Valley.

Abelmeholah and *Tabbath* are areas in the highlands across the Jordan.

The location of *Beth-barah* is unknown.

The reference to the gleaning of Ephraim means the mop-up work, finishing off the fleeing enemy.

Succoth is a rural rallying place located somewhere east of the Jordan.

Penuel (Peniel) is a city on the Jabbok east of the Jordan. This is the site of Jacob's struggle with the angel (Genesis 32:24-32).

Karkor is a spot well east of the Dead Sea near the Midianite home base. Gideon covers a bit of territory to catch those kings!

The location of *the pass of Heres* (NIV; NRSV = *ascent of Heres*) is unknown.

The Story Ends (8:22-35)

Impressed by Gideon's feats, the people ask him to rule as king. Gideon refuses, saying that God is Israel's ruler. However, Gideon then turns around and asks for gold from the booty to make an ephod. This priestly vestment had attached to it the breastplate of judgment. It was not only a magnificent garment; it was a symbol of authority, a symbol of the judge. Gideon may not be king, but he is pushing as close to kingship as he can get. Gideon is flirting with God's own place of authority.

The conflict between grasping and refusing power may have been Gideon's own, or it may reflect two writers' views of this great hero. The story's final version stresses the importance of recognizing God's supreme authority by noting that the ephod soon becomes an idol in itself and leads to the downfall of Gideon's family.

Verses 29 to 31 form a bridge to the story of Gideon's son, Abimelech. His life will carry his father's mistakes further. *Abimelech,* significantly, means *my father is king.*

The story ends on a tragic note. The judge, Gideon, has proved God's power. Yet Gideon's personal imperfection, his self-glorification, leads Israel back to a life of sin.

Ishmaelites is probably a generic term for nomad, rather

than a more specific reference to descendants of Abraham's son Ishmael.

Seventy sons is probably not a specific count of Gideon's offspring. Seventy was a politically significant number, indicating a full council.

Shechem was a Canaanite city and Baal cult center. Gideon's relationship with a Shechemite woman foreshadows Israel's trend back to idolatry.

§ § § § § § §

The Message of Judges 6–8

This section's major message is the basic Deuteronomic theme: God is the supreme authority, God is powerful, and God will save if the people will trust and obey. The story offers both a positive example (God's victory over Midian) and a negative example (the eventual ruin that came from Gideon's and Israel's failure to keep God in the place of honor).

There is another message, however, that is not stated directly. That is the idea that God can use not just good people but badly flawed ones as well. Gideon was originally fearful, lacking in faith, and doubtful that God even cared. Later he overstepped his commission and grasped at authority beyond his right. Yet God had used Gideon to save Israel.

With all our scientific accomplishments, it is easy for modern people to forget that it is not our own cleverness but the power of God that saves and sustains us. God is the world's supreme authority. Human attempts to usurp that authority can only lead us to disaster. Nevertheless, God will work with us as we are, flaws and all. The story of Gideon stands for us as an affirmation of God's powerful goodness and as a warning against the temptation of self-glorification.

§ § § § § § §

PART TWELVE Judges 9

Introduction to This Chapter

This story is different from most others in the book in that it is not a story about a judge. This is the story of a man who would lead, not by God's appointment, but at his own initiative. It is the story of Abimelech, Gideon's son. Gideon had refused the people's offer to crown him king. Abimelech was not so scrupulous. Although God was supposed to be Israel's only ruler, Abimelech set out to become a king. Abimelech was usurping God's authority, and he reaped a tragic harvest for his sin.

The story takes place in and around Shechem. Abimelech's mother was a Shechemite, so this was Abimelech's birthplace. It had a large Canaanite population and was an important center for Baal worship.

Shechem was centrally located in northern Israel and sat at the pass between Mount Ebal and Mount Gerizim. That made it an excellent place to establish a city-state. From there one could extend power in several directions. Abimelech may have had grand plans for an ever-enlarging kingdom.

Abimelech's lunge for power probably took place sometime between 1175 and 1150 B.C. We do not know when the original stories were first composed, but they could be quite old. Scholars can detect at least two strands of tradition within the present story, but the strands are thoroughly tied together now. The story probably appeared in the seventh-century Deuteronomic

90

90

history. From there it would take its place in the post-exilic history that we have today.

Chapter 9 does not begin with the usual formula concerning the Israelites doing evil, their crying out and the Lord sending a deliverer. The evil is obvious, but here there is no deliverer, so the formula would not fit. The story does support Deuteronomic attitudes and goals, however. The writer is openly contemptuous of Abimelech and carefully points out both his sins and his punishment.

Here is an outline of this chapter.
I. Kings of Shechem (9:1-6)
II. Jotham's Fable (9:7-21)
III. Quarrel and Rebellion (9:22-41)
IV. The Outcome (9:42-57)

King of Shechem (9:1-6)

Abimelech's first move is to approach his mother's family. He asks their help in promoting his campaign for kingship of Shechem. He then takes his pitch to the city fathers. There is no evidence that Abimelech's half-brothers live in Shechem or have any royal designs. But Abimelech offers the men of Shechem a choice between himself, with his Shechemite heritage, and all seventy of Gideon's sons as rulers. Given this somewhat dubious choice, the elders choose Abimelech. They bankroll him from the temple treasury. He hires a crew of thugs, then sets out to eliminate his "competition." He kills all his brothers except Jotham, who hides. Then he returns to be crowned king of Shechem.

The name *Abimelech* means *my father is king*. Gideon, a great military leader, was offered a kingship, but declined. He did, however, exercise extensive power and authority without the kingly title.

Jerubaal is Gideon's other name.

Baal-berith is lord of the covenant, a Canaanite god.

Scholars disagree on whether Beth-millo (verse 6) was an adjacent town, a place somehow related to Shechem's army, a fortress, or a pagan temple.

Jotham's Fable (9:7-21)

After the coronation, the remaining brother, Jotham, takes a prominent position on Mount Gerizim and delivers a speech. He tells a fable in which the trees have decided to choose a king. One by one the nominees decline. Each has a more important role to play in the community. Finally they ask the bramble, who accepts. The story is obviously meant to parallel Shechem's choice of Abimelech. So Jotham concludes with a warning to the people of Shechem: If they have dealt in good faith with Abimelech and with his father's house, then all should go well; if not, may they and Abimelech destroy each other. With that, Jotham flees. His words, however, will soon come tragically true.

There are complex translation problems here. Jotham was probably not on the actual mountain top, but on a prominent ledge part-way up. Archaeologists have found evidence of a non-Baalite gathering place on such a ledge.

Jotham's tree-symbol for Abimelech is the bramble, the only tree with nothing worthwhile to give. It does offer the others shade (protection), but what kind of shade can a bramble give to large trees? His promises are worthless! What's more, in a hot, dry place fire can break out in a bramble patch and spread to destroy even great cedars. This is the kind of "protection" Jotham predicts Abimelech will provide.

The men of Shechem have already paid for a massive slaughter of Jerubaal's (Gideon's) sons (*dealt well with Jerubaal* NRSV; NIV = *acted honorably and in good faith,* verse 16). This is how they have treated the family of a man who saved them from Midianite oppression. What they deserve is obvious.

The location of *Beer* is unknown.

Quarrel and Rebellion (9:22-41)

As so often happens, a relationship begun in treachery turns sour. The editor sees this as God's way of punishing all parties concerned.

Abimelech is living in Arumah, southeast of Shechem. Zebul serves as his deputy in the city. From Zebul Abimelech learns that public opinion is turning against him. The people are robbing travelers on the highway. This may be depriving Abimelech of lucrative turnpike or protection fees. The Shechemites have also set up an ambush for Abimelech himself. Soon an opportunist named Gaal has gained a following and plans a coup.

Zebul and Abimelech foil Gaal, however. Zebul maneuvers Gaal to the city gates. There he must face Abimelech and his army unprepared. Gaal flees, never to return.

Saying that Abimelech ruled Israel is an overstatement. He ruled only the small area around Shechem.

An *evil spirit* means bad feelings.

Little is known about Gaal. His name, however, combines elements meaning *to loathe* and *slave*. His father was an adherent of the corrupt temple in Shechem. From Israel's point of view Gaal would be a poor candidate for kingship.

Gaal compares Abimelech's mixed parentage (*Who is Abimelech?* verse 28) with his own pure Shechemite line as a way to gain leverage with the city elders.

The Hebrew word for *center of the land* (NIV; NRSV = *Tabbur-Erez*) means *navel*. This is a spot on Mount Gerizim thought to be the earth's center, the place where heaven and earth meet.

The Outcome (9:42-57)

The day after Gaal's defeat, Abimelech returns to Shechem. He slaughters a number of citizens in the fields, then destroys the city. From there he goes on to the town of Thebez, where he wreaks further destruction. He begins to burn the fortress tower as he has the one at Shechem, but this time a woman in the tower heaves out a millstone. The stone hits Abimelech, crushing his skull. The story ends with an editorial note that by their mutual destruction God has requited all the crimes of Abimelech and the men of Shechem.

The act of sowing with salt was intended to make the city perpetually desolate. The idea probably comes from the fact that nothing can grow in salted ground. The act may also be a symbolic implementation of a covenantal curse. If so, Abimelech is again pre-empting God's authority by doing this on his own.

El-berith is a variation of Baal-berith. The house of El-berith was apparently a temple that included a fortress-tower. This tower may have been outside the town, although that would be unusual.

The location of *Mount Zalmon* is uncertain, but it might be another name for Mount Ebal.

Thebez is a town about twelve miles northeast of Shechem. Possibly it had cooperated in Shechem's revolt against Abimelech.

A *millstone* is a large grinding stone. It would normally be too heavy for one person to lift. The woman may have had help getting it out the window.

Abimelech asks his armor-bearer to run him through with a sword so he will not die in disgrace, killed by a woman.

§ § § § § § §

The Message of Judges 9

Throughout the book of Judges the main message has been that those who trust and obey God, who affirm God's authority, will remain safe and prosperous. Here we see the negative side of that message. The writer presents Abimelech as a bad example. This young man has grasped at power, power that only God may exercise or confer. For this and related sins, Abimelech dies.

In today's technologically advanced, scientifically minded world, many people find it hard to recognize God's activity. It is easy to assume that we are in charge of things. Forgetting that this is God's world, we begin to make our own rules and behave however we choose toward other people and toward the environment. When we do this we can reap only disaster. No one—not Abimelech, not his modern counterparts—can get away with usurping God's authority.

§ § § § § § §

Judges 10–12

Introduction to These Chapters

Here we find accounts of six lesser-known judges. The
Deuteronomic editor apparently knew very little about
these men. Perhaps few significant events occurred in
their times. The story of just one, Jephthah, is told in
detail. He is the only one who faced and put down
oppression. The others ruled in peace, apparently serving
mainly as administrators. They saved Israel, not from
outside evil, but from internal disorder.

These judges served after the death of Abimelech. We
can't date Abimelech "reign" precisely, so we can't know
exactly when these six judges lived. It was probably
around the middle of the twelfth century B.C.

These chapters contain a mixture of old stories,
historical notes, and editorial comments. The notes about
five of the judges are very short. There is no mention of
the people doing evil or of any oppression. The usual
opening and closing formulas are absent. Those formulas
do occur, however, in the Jephthah story. There we see
again that the Israelites did evil which angered the Lord
and then they cried out to the Lord. When they did,
Jephthah was available to help them.

Here is an outline of these chapters:
  I. Tola (10:1-2)
 II. Jair (10:3-5)
III. Jephthah (10:6–12:7)
IV. Ibzan (12:8-10)

Tola (10:1-2)

Tola receives only this brief note in the book of Judges. Apparently he did nothing spectacular. Still, he was remembered over the centuries for his long and effective administration. Israel presumably remained at peace throughout his career. His home, Shamir, is probably a variant of Samaria.

Jair (10:3-5)

Another brief note tells of Jair. This judge, too, gave Israel peaceful administration. Jair was a judge on the east side of Jordan—he lived in Gilead, in the eastern territory of Manasseh, about 10 to 16 miles southeast of the Sea of Galilee.

Thirty sons and thirty towns suggest that Jair held extensive administrative responsibilities. The sons may be offspring or they may be chieftains under Jair's direction.

Thirty donkeys are an indication of prosperity.

Kamon is a town east of the Jordan on the road to Irbid.

Jephthah (10:6–12:7)

Jephthah was also from Gilead on the east side of the Jordan. He is the only judge of this group who was a military leader. He was, however, a man who tried to use diplomacy before war. He was also a man who kept his word, no matter what the cost.

These chapters include several stories and editorial notes tied together to make a continuous narrative. They begin with the classic formula's reference to the Israelites doing something evil. . . . Then we find a list of enemies and enemy gods. The whole list does not really apply to Jephthah's time. It is a summary of Israel's major enemies over a long period, both before and after Jephthah. The writer seems to be saying that any time powerful peoples threatened Israel, the Israelites were tempted to worship the enemies' gods.

When we actually get into Jephthah's story we find that oppression is coming from the Ammonites. These Ammonites were relative latecomers to the area. Sometime after Israel's settlement, the Ammonites had taken over the old Moabite territory far to the east of the Jordan. Now they were moving west into Israel's territory along the east bank of the Jordan and even into Israel's lands across the river.

Finally the people of Israel recognize their sin and cry to God for help. God expresses anger, but still cares. To show God's power and obvious concern, the writer lists the peoples from whom God has already saved Israel. This list again includes both past enemies and enemies who would not even arise until after Jephthah's time. But the point is made: God can and does save the people, yet the people lack both trust and gratitude. God suggests that the people should look for salvation to their new gods. But the people realize their error. So, God does save them.

The judge God uses is an unlikely candidate. In fact, it is embarrassing for the tribal leaders to ask his help. Jephthah, an illegitimate child, has been banished. He has to be brought back from another town. Jephthah agrees to take both military and civil leadership. God ratifies the agreement between Jephthah and his native tribe.

Jephthah first tries diplomacy with the Ammonites. He offers a reasoned argument for Israel's claim to the east bank territory. Israel had taken it centuries before from the Amorites. The Ammonites had not questioned this settlement for 300 years. Why should they start fighting over it now? Besides, the Ammonites already had ample territory to the east. Why not stay there in peace as their Moabite predecessors had?

The Ammonites do not accept Israel's argument, and

war ensues. In preparing for battle, Jephthah makes a rash vow to God. He wins the fight. So, on his return home, he must fulfill his vow—he must sacrifice the first living thing that comes out of his house. That turns out to be his only child. True to his word, Jephthah does sacrifice her. The storyteller seems to both applaud Jephthah's integrity and mourn his tragedy. Human sacrifice was not acceptable in Israel, yet a vow to God was sacred. No one would dare trifle with the Deity by failing to honor a vow.

Next Jephthah, like Gideon before him, must deal with an angry group of Ephraimites (see Judges 8:1-3).

Jephthah has crossed the river into Ephraimite territory to clean out the Ammonites there. The Ephraimites claim they weren't informed or called to help; Jephthah says that he had asked for help earlier but the Ephraimites did not respond. Again Jephthah tries to argue his opponents out of fighting, but they refuse. A battle ensues, Israelite tribe against Israelite tribe. Jephthah overcomes the Ephraimites. As they try to flee back across the Jordan, Jephthah's men stop them. The Gileadites apply a test. Any man who claims he is not an Ephraimite must say the word "Shibboleth." If he cannot pronounce it correctly, he is proved an Ephraimite and must die. Thus the complaining Ephraimite band is virtually wiped out.

With peace finally established, Jephthah continues to administer the Gilead area until his death.

Gilead is a sub-group of the eastern Manasseh tribe.

The *Amorites* are Canaanites. Some live in Judah; others live east of the Jordan.

The *Ammonites* are an aggressive tribe living east of the Jordan.

Maon is a town in the hill district of southern Judah. Maonites could be Edomite inhabitants of this town, or they could be members of a larger confederation from the east to which Maon belonged. Maonites were prominent enemies of Israel at a much later time, around 873–849 B.C.

Sidonians are residents of a city on the Mediterranean. These, too, fought against Israel somewhat later.

Philistines are a group living along the Mediterranean coast. They appear prominently in the Samson and David stories.

Amalekites are nomads who roamed over much of Palestine, often collaborating with Israel's enemies.

Gilead was the father of Jephthah (11:1) may simply mean that Jephthah was a Gileadite. Or, it may suggest that the tribe was his father. In other words, his individual father was not known.

Tob is either a city in Syria or a town about fifteen miles east of Ramoth-gilead.

Three hundred years is a round number roughly indicating the whole period of the judges up to this time.

The coming of the *Spirit of the* LORD was the sign of a true judge.

Mizpah (verse 29) is not Mizpah of the west, but a town of unknown location in Gilead.

In verse 31, *whoever comes out* (NRSV) might also read *whatever comes out* (NIV). Animals could be sheltered in Jephthah's house, and he could be assuming that some animal would wander out for his sacrifice.

Zaphon is near the east bank of the Jordan, probably between Succoth and Zarethan.

Ibzan (12:8-10)

No more than this is known of Ibzan. He apparently administered Israel in times of peace. The thirty sons suggest heavy administrative responsibilities. His ability to arrange so many marriages suggests that he had good relationships with neighboring tribes. Ibzan's home, Bethlehem, is a northern town in Zebulun, not the southern town of David and Jesus.

Elon (12:11-12)

Elon was also from Zebulun. The writer apparently had very little information about him. He, too, ruled in peace; at least, he fought no battles worth noting. His name means *oak* or *terebinth* (another large tree). Aijalon's location is uncertain. The name, however, could be an alternate spelling of Elon, so there could be some confusion here between the judge's name and his burial place.

Abdon (12:13-15)

This is another little-known judge who apparently ruled in peace. Pirathon was probably about six miles west of Shechem. Forty sons and thirty grandsons would make a standard council of seventy. This was a large clan for which Abdon was responsible. The seventy donkeys again suggest prosperity. Abdon could afford to provide donkeys for all his subordinates.

§ § § § § § §

The Message of Judges 10–12

The basic message of the Jephthah story is the familiar Judges theme: when people sin, they suffer; when they turn to God, God can and will save them. The message of the remaining notices is an implicit rather than an explicit variation of this basic theme. The brief notes with little comment suggest that during these years the people did not sin and thus were able to live peacefully under a God-given judge. These notes also suggest that good administration is a gift of God just as much as is a more dramatic military victory.

To us these passages may be saying that God provides for the chosen people in many ways. When necessary God may save us in a dramatic way from our enemies. At other times God may keep us safe by the gift of good, steady leadership. Whatever the situation, the blessings of safety, freedom, and peace come from a good, powerful, and caring God. They are available to us when we remain faithful and obedient.

§ § § § § § §

Introduction to These Chapters

These are the stories of Samson. Samson was a man chosen before birth to be God's instrument in freeing Israel. He was not what we would consider a perfect candidate. He was headstrong, hot-tempered, not very smart, and unwilling or unable to learn from his mistakes. He had a weakness for women and blundered into all sorts of trouble. Yet, in God's Spirit, this man had magnificent physical strength. God used that strength to subdue large numbers of the foreigners who were ruling over Israel.

The stories take place in Judah, in southern Dan, and in the southern Philistine territory near the Mediterranean Sea. Samson's home is on the border between Judah and Dan, about fourteen miles west of Jerusalem.

The enemy Israel faces is Philistia. The Philistines had entered Palestine around 1200 B.C. They had settled along the seacoast, then proceeded to push progressively inland. Slowly they inched ever farther into Israel's territory. By the time of Samson (1150–1100 B.C.) the Philistines had apparently moved into much of southern Palestine. At first they were not heavy-handedly oppressive, but in later years Israel would frequently have to fight off Philistine armies. The memory of these violent encounters may have added to the storytellers' obvious glee in relating their tales of Philistine defeat.

These chapters include several stories and even an ancient poem or victory song. Unlike some parts of Judges, this section contains very little editorial comment. That may be because the stories were so old and so well known that they were set in the public mind. The editor would not then feel so free to add his own comments. The cycle does begin, however, with the standard Deuteronomic formula, concerning the Israelites doing evil according to God. The rest of the formula, *the people cried . . . and the* LORD *raised up a judge,* is missing.

The incidents recorded here are excellent examples of ancient storytelling. They are highly entertaining, suspenseful, and skillfully constructed so that climactic events are set up in advance yet held back just enough to retain the listener's attention. As in most folk literature, we find here some very effective exaggeration. Samson's feats of strength and the number of Philistines killed are fantastic. Yet the exaggeration does not mean that the stories lack historical roots. It simply means that the storytellers playfully "poked their listeners in the ribs" a little to make the point stick.

Modern readers may be somewhat surprised to find here a biblical hero whose morals are distressingly low. Samson's visits to prostitutes and wanton murder of innocent men in Ashkelon do not match our expectations of a religious figure. What's more, the writers and editors do not criticize Samson's behavior. We must, however, consider the times in which Samson lived. Apparently this behavior was not unusual. And, because the stories were so firmly set, later editors neither condemned nor brushed up Samson's brutality and looseness. Instead they allowed his imperfections to focus the spotlight completely on God's power. In effect they said, "Here is a man in all his weakness. See how God has been able to use him."

Here is an outline of these chapters.

The Story Begins (13:1-25)

The writer opens with his usual formula. Then he moves right into the ancient story.

An angel appears to a barren woman announcing that she will soon bear a son who will someday save Israel. The mother must observe strict prenatal instructions because this child is to be a Nazirite from conception. She must keep all the Nazirite rules to avoid compromising her child's purity. Her husband, Manoah, requests and receives additional verification of the message. Finally the son, Samson, is born. Very early God's Spirit (proof of divine election) stirs in the child).

Zorah is a town fourteen miles west of Jerusalem, on the border between Judah and Dan.

A *Nazirite* is a person consecrated to God for a period of time, not necessarily a lifetime. Later Nazirites kept three rules. They did not cut their hair, they abstained from wine and other alcoholic beverages, and they avoided contact with dead or unclean flesh. These are the rules given to Samson's mother. Other older accounts do not mention avoidance of the dead.

Manoah asks for verification because a woman's word is not considered reliable.

The angel says that his name is *wonderful* (NRSV), beyond *understanding* (NIV), as is his entire being.

Samson is a Canaanite name. The meaning of the name is unclear.

Mahanehdan is a camp of Dan.

Eshtaol is a town located about a mile from the village of Zorah.

A Stormy Marriage (14:1–15:8)

In this next story Samson is a young man. He is already quite headstrong. Hebrew parents usually chose their children's spouses. However, Samson has taken a shine to a Philistine girl from Timnah. He decides to marry her against his parents' wishes. They, of course, are concerned because she is not of their people and does not worship their God. She is, in fact, a member of the nation that is taking over Israel. Samson, however, goes ahead. He makes his own wedding arrangements. In one of the story's few editorial remarks (14:4), someone has explained this odd marriage as God's way of arranging a situation where Samson will get into a fight with the Philistines.

On a trip to Timnah we see the first sign of Samson's great strength. He tears a lion apart with his bare hands. On the next trip he finds honey in the carcass. That honey provides the lead-in to a riddle on which the rest of the story hangs.

Now the seven-day wedding feast begins. Samson makes a bet that that the guests cannot answer a riddle. On the fourth day the guests approach the bride for help in learning the answer. Her tears and pleading melt the foolish Samson. So, on the final feast day the guests spring their response. Samson must pay up.

But he does not have the sixty garments required. The marriage legalities are incomplete (all would be ratified at the end of the seventh day), but Samson angrily stomps off. He goes twenty miles to Ashkelon, kills thirty Philistines, and brings back two garments from each to give the guests. Then he leaves.

The bride's surprised and embarrassed parents promptly marry the girl to the best man. Some time later, Samson returns to find his bride married. In anger he burns the Philistines' crops. The Philistines take their vengeance on the bride's family. Samson retaliates with a huge slaughter. He then goes into hiding.

Timnah is a city on the northern border of Judah. It would be about four miles southwest of Mahanehdan.

Ashkelon is a Philistine town on the Mediterranean Sea.

The Israelites saw circumcision as a sign of their dedication to God. Philistines did not practice circumcision.

The honey may foreshadow Samson's role as a strong fighter. Mesopotamians used honey in preparation for battle. Israelites believed honey produced enlightenment and courage. Here, ironically, this very substance plays a major part in Samson's first downfall.

She wept seven days (verse 17) is an error. Obviously she wept only four of the seven days.

The bride's father tries vainly to placate this dangerous, angry man by offering him another daughter, a *younger sister*.

The *cleft (cave) of rock of Etam* is a hiding place in the rocks near Samson's home.

Confrontation with the Philistines (15:9-20)

The retaliatory cycle continues. The Philistines come after Samson. Fearing reprisals, the men of Judah determine to turn him over. He agrees, assuming that he can easily fight off the Philistines anyway. He meets them, snaps his bonds, grabs a handy jawbone, and uses it to kill a thousand men. Then this fearless fighter suddenly realizes that he is thirsty and grows afraid that he may be weakened. God, however, opens a rock where Samson finds water.

The bone and water incidents are two examples of a common type of biblical literature, the story that explains or is verbally connected with the name of a place.

Linguistic analysis indicates that Samson's song (verse 16) is a very ancient one.

Lehi means *jawbone*.

Three thousand are a lot of men. The Judahites had great respect for Samson's strength!

A *fresh jawbone* would be much stronger than a dry, brittle, old one.

Ramath-lehi means *hill of the jawbone*. The battle took place on high ground.

En-hakkore means *mortar*. This was a hollow stone in the shape of a mortar. Water may have collected there, or the stone may have held a small spring. Water from a rock recalls a similar experience of Moses (see Exodus 17).

Temptations, Defeat, and Victory (16:1-31)

Here we find two more stories of Samson's prodigious strength.

First Samson goes off to the Philistine city of Gaza, where he visits a harlot. Realizing he is dangerous, the men of Gaza determine to capture him. Apparently, though, they fall asleep during the evening. At midnight Samson decides to leave the locked city. So, he pulls up the gates and carries them all the way to Hebron.

Next Samson goes to the Valley of Sorek, where he meets and moves in with Delilah. The Philistine men bribe her to learn the secret of Samson's strength. Delilah wheedles and nags at Samson. At first he puts her off with phony stories. But finally female pleas again undo him. Perhaps trusting too much in his physical strength, he tells her his strength lies in his hair. Actually, his special Nazirite commitment is the source of his strength. Cutting off the hair would end that commitment. And, without the commitment he would not have strength from God. But Samson may never have taken his Nazirite status seriously. He has ignored the prohibitions against strong drink and touching dead bodies already. (The last, however, may not have been a requirement in Samson's time.) Now Samson rather lightly breaks the last vow and, to his surprise, loses his strength. The Philistines bind and blind him.

Still, God is able to use Samson one last time. The Philistines, celebrating his capture, proceed to make great fun of him. In the intervening time, however, Samson's hair has been growing back. Samson calls upon God to strengthen him once more. Then, in God's Spirit, Samson pulls down the temple pillars, killing thousands of Philistines and himself. In death he is avenged.

Gaza is a Philistine city of southwest Palestine about thirty-eight miles south of Zorah.

Hebron is an Israelite city in southeast Palestine. It is thirty-eight miles east of Gaza.

The large metal *city gate* would be imbedded in stone posts with two-story guardhouses on either side. The Gazite men may have spent the night inside the guardhouses and so would not hear Samson soon enough to prevent his escape.

The *Valley of Sorek* is a grape-growing area near Zorah.

The name *Delilah* means *flirtatious*.

1,100 pieces (shekels) of silver is a huge amount of money.

The *fabric on a loom* (NIV) are called a *web* (NRSV).

Dagon is an ancient Mesopotamian god whose worship had spread into Palestine.

3,000 on the roof is the storyteller's exaggerated version of a great many people.

§ § § § § § §

The Message of Judges 13–16

The Samson stories provide yet another variation on the basic Deuteronomic message that God is the source of saving strength for Israel. Samson is not a hero in himself. In fact, on his own he is a bumbling, hot-tempered fool. Yet God can use a man like Samson to free the people.

The stories also illustrate a converse message. Breaking the covenant relationship with God cuts one off from God's strength. Samson, in allowing his hair to be cut, broke his Nazirite vow. He broke his relationship with God and lost the strength that came from God.

The story's dramatic ending offers another basic Deuteronomic message: When people turn and call upon God, God does come to them and save them.

Beneath the human interest and excitement of the Samson tales the writer has given us once again his essential theological word: If we remain in right relationship with God, God will strengthen and save us. If not, we will suffer. Modern people, as much as their ancient counterparts, need to recognize these basic truths if we, collectively and as individuals, are to survive.

§ § § § § § §

Judges 17–18

Introduction to These Chapters

These and the remaining chapters form a kind of appendix to the book of Judges. They are historical reminiscences from the same general time period, but they do not narrate stories of particular judges. The stories lack the usual Deuteronomic formula. There is no note of Israel's sin, of outside oppression, of a cry for help, or of God's provision for a hero-judge to save the people. These chapters are simply additional bits of history that the editor apparently did not want to leave out.

The story in chapters 17–18 seems to have been composed for a particular purpose: to explain why for many years Levitical priests maintained an illegitimate sanctuary in Dan. The story's development involves events in the lives of a man from Ephraim, a Levite from Judah, and a large portion of the tribe of Dan. These three elements converge because of some religious paraphernalia. As the tale unfolds, the Ephraimite sets up a worship center and hires the Levite to tend it. At that point, the Ephraimite loses the worship center to thieving Danites, who are in the process of moving to new territory. Like many portions of Judges, this is a good example of ancient storytelling.

These events take place around 1100–1050 B.C. At that time Philistine pressure was squeezing the Danites out of their allotted territory. The religious and social situation reflected here suggests that the story itself may come from a time near the events described.

The story's age could help explain a factor that may seem odd to modern readers. That is the biblical storyteller's apparent unconcern for the morality (or immorality) of his characters. The story tells of theft, image-making (which is expressly forbidden and roundly criticized in other texts), and the slaughter of innocent people. The storyteller makes no explicit comment on any of this. Neither does any editor. Only the story itself and two brief bits of editorial information offer any possible hint of justice for these wrongs. Such an attitude could reflect the less-sensitive morality of an earlier age. By the time the editors incorporated this material it would be so entrenched in the popular mind that additional comment would be difficult, and perhaps unnecessary, to include.

On the surface, these chapters do little to promote the writer's particular theological concerns, but he apparently chose to preserve them, basically unaltered, as part of his people's heritage.

Here is an outline of these chapters.
  I. Micah's Story (17:1-13)
 II. The Danites' Move (18:1-13)
III. The Danites and Micah Clash (18:14-26)
 IV. Settlement at Laish (18:27-31)

Micah's Story (17:1-13)

As the story begins, an Ephraimite, Micah, has stolen 1,100 pieces of silver from his mother. Possibly because he is frightened by the curse she has put on the silver, Micah confesses and returns the money to her. His mother consecrates the silver to make images for the worship of God. Micah sets up a shrine, with his son as priest.

Some time later, a Levite who is looking for work

comes by. Micah hires him to replace the son as priest. He hopes that having a "real" priest will improve his fortunes.

Micah is not the later prophet Micah. Rather, this Micah is an otherwise unknown man from the tribe of Ephraim. The name Micah is short for Micayehu, which means *who is like or comparable to Yahweh (God)*? Later listeners would probably catch an ironic contrast between this man's pious name and his questionable religious and moral life.

Ephraim is a tribe located in the central part of Palestine, north of Judah and north of Dan's original territory.

1,100 pieces (shekels) of silver is a great deal of money. Each of the Philistine men offered Delilah this amount to betray Samson (Judges 16:5).

In verse 4, it is unclear at first whether the *carved image and a cast idol* (NIV; NRSV = *an idol of cast metal*, is one molded and engraved image or two images. In 18:17, however, there are clearly two images. These were not pagan idols but images intended for the worship of God, although Exodus 20:4 forbids any kind of image.

An *ephod* is a religious vestment worn during religious ceremonies.

Teraphim (NRSV) are small *idols* (NIV). The Babylonians used these to foretell events or to discern the will of the gods. This seems to have been one function of Micah's shrine. (See 18:5-6.)

The comment that there was *no king* underscores Israel's loose organization at this time. There was no one in authority who was empowered to make nationwide rules, so each one had to make his own. Micah and the Levite obviously did so.

Levites were normally members of the tribe of Levi, who were set aside to serve as priests. They did not receive a particular territorial allotment, but were assigned certain cities scattered throughout Palestine

(Joshua 21). *Levites* may sometimes, however, have designated a person who served as a priest but was a member of another tribe. This might explain the strange description of a Levite *from Bethlehem in Judah.* Another possibility is that the author meant simply that this Levite *had been living within the clan of Judah* (NIV). We do not know why this Levite was looking for another place to work. Perhaps there were too many Levites in Bethlehem, or perhaps he simply wanted a change.

The Danites' Move (18:1-13)

Now we turn to a seemingly unrelated situation. Dan has been assigned land between Judah and Ephraim (Joshua 19:40-46). The tribe has not been strong enough to hold this land, however, so the group decides to move. Five spies travel north looking for a spot. On the way, these spies stop at Micah's house. They ask the Levite for a sign concerning their mission. The Levite assures them that God is with them. At Laish they find a peaceful, prosperous, and defenseless people. Most of the people of Dan then set out to take this area. As they travel north, the whole group stops at Micah's house.

In biblical Hebrew, the name *Dan* means *judgment.* Unknowingly, the tribe of Dan does visit judgment upon Micah. But the writer does not make an explicit point of this outcome.

Zorah and *Eshtaol* are two towns on the border between Dan and Judah. Over the years there was some confusion as to which tribe held them. In Joshua 15:33 the towns are assigned to Judah. Zorah is noted as the home of Samson (Judges 13:2).

Recognized the voice (verse 3): Perhaps they recognized the Levite's accent or realized there was Levite about when they head him chanting.

Laish is a city about 100 miles north of Micah's home. The name means *lion.*

Sidonians were inhabitants of Sidon, a Phoenician city

on the Mediterranean. The people of Laish were of Phoenician stock but, living so far inland, they were isolated from their relatives. Thus, they would receive no help from outside.

Kiriath-jearim is a town about 8 miles northwest of Jerusalem.

Mahanehdan is a camp of the tribe of Dan. In this story it is at Kiriath-jearim. As a camp, however, it may have moved around. It is not necessarily in the same location as the camp mentioned in the Samson story (Judges 13:25).

The Danites and Micah Clash (18:14-26)

The Danite spies, remembering Micah's shrine, suggest that the tribe take his religious equipment. The tribe agrees. The spies also convince the Levite to come with them by offering him a job promotion. Now he can be priest to a whole tribe, not just one family or village. Micah tries to recover his gods, but the Danites are too strong for him.

The Levite's character is rather interesting—he will apparently do anything to get ahead. But the storyteller makes no point of this nor does any later editor. Perhaps they expect the listener's own sense of right and wrong to provide judgment.

The point of putting the *little ones* (NRSV; NIV = *children*) . . . *in front* is to put the warriors in back to protect both families and images from a rear attack by Micah.

Settlement at Laish (18:27-31)

The Danites attack Laish without warning, slaughtering its unsuspecting inhabitants. Then they rebuild the city and rename it Dan. They set up a sanctuary with Micah's images and install the Levite to preside over it. Thus the story ends.

Apparently tradition held that the priests at Dan were

descendants of Moses' grandson, Jonathan. The text seems to say that the previously unidentified Levite was actually this Jonathan.

Captivity of the land means either the Assyrian conquest of 733 B.C. or the forced removal of the Danites from the area in 721 B.C. The point is just a small historical note, with no comment or criticism attached. The fact could, however, suggest to later listeners a punishment for Danite sin.

Shiloh is a city in Ephraim located about ten miles northeast of Bethel. For many years Shiloh housed a major Israelite temple. That temple was destroyed about 1060 B.C.

§ § § § § § §

The Message of Judges 17–18

Actually, this story carries no explicit message. Listeners or readers are left to determine the meaning for themselves. Listeners of a later time would probably take an "isn't it too bad?" attitude toward the setting up of images and independent sanctuaries. Yet, there are only two historical notes that might vaguely suggest editorial disapproval.

The story does, however, imply a basic Deuteronomic message. The message is that the person who sins will eventually suffer. That is clearly what happens in Micah's case. He originally steals some silver. In the end, his silver idols are stolen from him. The case of the Danites is not so certain. It depends on whether or not that brief mention of the "captivity" was meant to suggest a punishment.

The modern reader can perhaps take from Judges 17–18 this thought: that evil tends to bring evil back to the perpetrator. Recompense may not always be immediate or obvious, but wrong actions set in motion other wrongs that can eventually come back to us.

§ § § § § § §

Introduction to These Chapters

This section, along with chapters 17–18, forms an appendix to the book of Judges. The story belongs to the Judges time period. This is not, however, the story of a judge. It is the story of an evil event that led to civil war and the near devastation of the tribe of Benjamin. Even though it is not the usual "judge" story, the writer has apparently preserved this account in order to offer as complete an historical record as possible.

These chapters include several distinct traditions and editorial notes. In some spots we can see that a later editor or storyteller needed to give his listeners extra information to explain points of a very old tale. The final editor, however, has skillfully woven the parts together to form an exciting and coherent narrative.

The story lacks the usual Deuteronomic formula noting Israel's sin, the oppression it brought, Israel's cry for help, and God's gift of a judge. This standard structure would not fit the situation at all. Instead, it begins and ends with the simple comment, *In those days there was no king in Israel* (NRSV; NIV = *Israel had no king*).

We do find here, as in many ancient tales, some skillful storytelling techniques, including occasional exaggeration for effect. Still, much of this material deals with a real historical event. Certainly the story accurately depicts Israel's political situation at the time. We see here a leaderless people divided, tribe against tribe, trying to wrestle with major problems of justice, order, and unity.

Mob action, unaided by previously formed policies or institutions, leads Israel to the brink of disaster.

The story, ancient and reworked as it is, offers a curious mix of moral attitudes. The lack of hospitality, the threat of homosexual attack on a guest, the gang rape and murder receive the label "abomination." The authors and editors, however, say nothing about the offering of two women to placate the mob, the slaughter of women and children in Jabesh-gilead, or the kidnapping of wives for the Benjaminites. We would hesitate to draw conclusions about Israel's morality from this story, except to say that it offers an interesting peek into the development of moral sensitivity. Later editors' hesitation to change or comment on the story does not necessarily mean that they shared the story's earlier attitudes.

Here is an outline of these chapters.
  I. The Levite's Story (19:1-30)
 II. Israel's Response (20:1-48)
III. Making Peace Again (21:1-25)

The Levite's Story (19:1-30)

The story begins with a common Judges formula noting that in those days, Israel did not have a king. This simple statement places the events in the time before the monarchy. It may also, however, be meant to convey the tragedy of Israel's anarchic situation and/or the idea that in those days God alone was king. In any case, this opening effectively suggests the kind of inter-tribal chaos we will soon see in detail.

We next learn of an unnamed Levite who is returning with his concubine from Judah to his home in Ephraim. Late in the afternoon he reaches Jerusalem, where his servant suggests they spend the night. Ironically the Levite refuses because this is a foreign city. (Israel did not control Jerusalem until much later.) He prefers to go on to Gibeah in Benjamin where he expects greater hospitality among Israelites. Unfortunately he will receive there worse treatment than any foreigners would be likely to give.

In Gibeah there are no hotels, yet no one will take the Levite in, even though his servant, donkeys, and goods indicate his prosperity. Finally an old Ephraimite living in the town extends an invitation. Soon, however, some of the Gibeonite men arrive, demanding the Levite as an object for attack. The Ephraimite, determined to protect his guest, offers the men both the Levite's concubine and his own virgin daughter. The men refuse. Finally, however, the Levite pushes the concubine out and the men spend the night raping her.

By morning the woman is dead. The Levite carries her body home, cuts it into twelve pieces, and sends the pieces out among the twelve tribes of Israel.

A *Levite* is a priest, a member of the tribe of Levi. This tribe had no territorial claim but lived in cities throughout Palestine.

To *sojourn* means to stay for a time. A sojourner was a person who lived among people not of his or her own tribe.

A *concubine* is a slave purchased as a wife.

Jebus is another name for Jerusalem. It lies five to six miles north of Bethlehem.

Gibeah is a town in Benjamin four miles north of Jerusalem. At the time of this story Gibeah was surrounded by Canaanite settlements. Canaanite influence may have led to the Gibeonites abominable behavior.

Ramah is a town about six miles north of Jerusalem.

Throughout the Middle East, hospitality to a traveler was a sacred duty. In Gibeah, however, no Benjaminite would invite the Levite in. Only a man from Ephraim would offer him the customary politeness.

In verse 22, men from that city demand to have sexual

intercourse with the guest. For a similar situation see the attack on Lot's guests at Sodom (Genesis 19).

The guest-host relationship was a sacred one. The host was to ensure the guest's safety and well-being; the guest was bound to do no harm to the host. If the Gibeonite men were to succeed in their plans, the host would be gravely at fault for failing to protect his guest.

The offer of his daughter and the concubine is the Ephraimite's last wild attempt to avoid the sin of failing to protect a guest. Women, even women one cared for very much, were dispensable. The Levite, however, finally prevents harm to his host's child by shoving his concubine out to the men.

In verse 29, pieces of the concubine's body are sent to different areas of Israel. An animal cut in pieces was a signal used to mobilize the tribes for a fight.

Israel's Response (20:1-48)

An army assembles. The Levite tells his story, with slight alterations to put his own part in the best light. The Israelites, enraged by the Gibeonite crime, seek revenge. First, they ask the Benjaminites to give up the guilty men. The Benjaminites stubbornly determine to defend their own. A three-day battle ensues. For two days the Benjaminites prevail. On the third day, however, the Israelites divide their forces. As they had done at Ai long ago (Joshua 8), one force feigns retreat to draw the enemy out of the city. Then a second, hidden force sets fire to the city and attacks the enemy from behind. The defeated Benjaminites flee northeastward to the cave-pocked cliffs at Rimmon.

The story of this mini-war may combine two or more versions. Verses 37-44 in particular seem to be a separate, older account.

The extent of Israel's territory in David's time was from *Dan to Beersheba*.

Mizpah is the scene of an ancient shrine near Gibeah.

This town is not to be confused with the Mizpah located east of the Jordan.

Four hundred thousand is a large army. Numbers in this story should probably not be taken literally.

The Israelites cast lots to see which tribe would go first into battle.

The extended battle serves to heighten suspense. The two defeats may also serve to weed out Israel's forces so that God, not a superior military force, might receive credit for the final victory.

Being *left-handed* may have been a special peculiarity among Benjaminites. Ehud (Judges 3:15) was left-handed. First Chronicles 12:2 also speaks of Benjaminites using both right and left hands.

Bethel is a city north of Gibeah on the boundary between Ephraim and Benjamin. Bethel was the scene of an important shrine. The ark (container) of the covenant was normally kept at Shiloh. However, in this story the sacred object is at Bethel.

Inquire of the Lord means to ask God's guidance. Israel does not do so before deciding on revenge. The people do seek some advice before entering battle, however. Note that God only answers the questions the people ask. God does not promise victory until the third day.

At the book's end, as in chapter 1, Judah is the first to go into battle. It is possible that the writer included this detail for literary balance.

The location of *Baal-tamar* is unknown.

The eastern hills are called the *wilderness*.

In verse 33, *Geba* is either a town on the way to Rimmon (NRSV) or a variation of *Gibeah* (NIV).

In verse 43, *Nohah,* only referred to in the NRSV, is a site named for one of the clans of Benjamin. Its location is unknown.

Rimmon is a limestone outcrop dotted with caves three to four miles east of Bethel.

The exact location of *Gidom* is unknown.

Making Peace Again (21:1-25)

This conclusion to the story (and the book) focuses on Israel's resourcefulness and unity despite internal strife.

The Israelites now have their revenge. Justice has been done. But what a price has been paid! Too late the Israelites realize that they have all but destroyed one of their own twelve tribes. The war has not only killed many men, but has left almost no Benjaminite women with whom the surviving soldiers could mate and rebuild the tribe. Worse yet, the other tribes had rashly vowed not to give their daughters in marriage to Benjaminites. Now the storyteller really has his listeners on cliff's edge!

But the resourceful Israelites do find a way out. The tribes had taken another sacred vow. That was to punish any group that did not join in the war. There is one city that did not participate: Jabesh-gilead. (This city had some previous marital ties with Benjamin.) The Israelites promptly attack Jabesh-gilead and kill everyone except the town's 400 young girls. These girls they turn over to the Benjaminites as a gesture of peace.

Still, 400 girls are not enough. So the Israelites devise another plan. Let the Benjaminites steal more wives at the Shiloh festival. The Benjaminites do so, the fathers of Shiloh do not break their vow by giving their daughters to Benjaminites, and the rift between the tribes is healed. No one apparently cares about the girls or about the innocent women and children killed at Jabesh-gilead. They are not the focal point of the story. The maintenance of justice and unity in faithfulness to God is the goal, and listeners can heave a sigh of relief when Israel finally achieves that goal.

The story and the whole book of Judges end with the statement about the absence of a king in Israel. This statement sums up the political reality of the judges' period. It may also suggest that tragic strife like the Benjaminite war is what happens when there is neither earthly king nor careful following of Israel's divine king.

Yet despite Israel's folly, that divine king has made everything come out right.

To ancient Hebrews a sacred vow had great power. If broken, the vow would bring a terrible curse or even death upon the offender. Thus the Israelites could not consider breaking their vows under any circumstances.

Jabesh-gilead is a city east of the Jordan in the territory of Gilead.

Shiloh is a city in Ephraim north of Bethel. Shiloh was the site of a major Israelite temple.

§ § § § § § §

The Message of Judges 19–21

The writer gives no explicit interpretation to this story. Rather, the story itself shows a problem and points to a solution. The problem is how to provide justice and still maintain unity within the people of God. Israel's rather fumbling answer here was to provide justice, then find a way to heal the breach made in the process. Punish, then forgive and aid in recovery was their solution. Through all this, even though the tribes were disorganized and leaderless, they received support from their true king, God.

This message was especially important for Israel in the time of the Exile. Leaderless and broken, angry with each other and throwing blame right and left, the people needed to know that God could heal and unite their tribes once more.

Today, in our families and in our world, we face the double need to enforce right behavior while maintaining unity. We hope to find less brutal methods than Israel did for accomplishing this. Nevertheless, as we walk that tightrope between righteous indignation and healing forgiveness, we can rest assured of God's aid and support. God, in infinite power, can mend the breaks in our fractured world.

§ § § § § § §

Introduction to Ruth

Introduction to the Book of Ruth

The book of Ruth is a historical short story. It is a love story of the conventional man-woman kind. But it is also a love story in a broader sense. This Old Testament book is a story of many good people who love and care for each other. And, beneath it all, this is a love story about God.

In Ruth, love and concern are everywhere. There is not an unkind person or a villain in the piece. There are only ordinary people showing love to family members and, beyond the family, to strangers. In this superb tale we meet unforgettable characters like Naomi, a grieving widow who looks after the interests of her daughters-in-law; Ruth, who leaves home and risks her safety to care for Naomi; and Boaz, who shows kindness to the foreigner, Ruth, and eventually marries her. Behind the scenes, guiding and protecting, we see a God whose love is stronger and broader than many humans may have suspected.

Purpose and Date

Ruth is intended to be both entertaining and instructive. One of the book's major purposes is to show that God wants people to live in self-giving love. But the author apparently had another, more specific, purpose: to deal with the problem of how Israel should relate to foreigners. Over and over the author reminds us that

Ruth is from Moab, that she is a foreigner. Yet she and the other characters treat each other with love. In that light Ruth is a love story with wide social significance—a story of love between nations and groups, between people with differences who share the same parent-child relationship with God.

This second purpose probably arose from the historical situation in which the author lived. Both the language and content suggest that the story as it now stands comes from 450-250 B.C. This was a time after the Exile when Nehemiah and others were trying very hard to preserve Israel's unity and purity by limiting the people's relationships with outsiders. They strictly enforced the traditional rule forbidding intermarriage with foreigners (Nehemiah 10:28-31). They emphasized the law in Deuteronomy 23:3 that forbids foreigners from fully entering the Israelite community. Some saw foreigners as evil, inferior, or both. To many, God seemed to be God of Israel alone. Ruth's author opposed this exclusivism. But instead of writing a diatribe, he wrote a brilliantly gentle story—a story in which a loving Moabite woman marries an Israelite and eventually becomes the ancestress of Israel's greatest king.

The story itself may be a very old one. Its cultural details accurately reflect the Judges period. It contains many ancient words as well. So it seems likely that the author has taken a beloved old story and used it to make an effective point about a situation in his own time.

While most commentators agree on the book's purpose, a few do not place the author in the post-exilic time period. Some scholars argue that much of the language could come from the monarchic period, and that concern for inclusiveness could have arisen before the Exile. If this were the case, Ruth's date of composition could be set at the time of Jehoshaphat's reform in the second quarter of the ninth century B.C.

However, these arguments do not seem compelling. Instead, the exilic setting still seems the more likely one.

Theology

God, in the book of Ruth, is a God who actively cares for people. However, God works in the shadows. Occasionally God's presence is noted directly. More often, though, we hear of God through the blessings and prayers of the story's characters.

The author assumes that God is behind the good things that happen—the famine's end, the "luck" that brings Ruth to Boaz's field, and so forth. We are led to feel that God is working toward good even when evil seems dominant.

In this story God acts most often through people. They are ordinary people in ordinary circumstances. Yet they are good people, good as God is good. They live in imitation of God and, in so doing, fulfill the plans of God.

The happy ending makes one final theological point: that God will reward righteous, godly living. This is no rigid legalism, however. The author suggests that happiness will eventually come to those who love and give. The greatest happiness comes to those who love and give beyond what is legally required.

The Author

We know nothing about the author of Ruth except what we can guess from the story he wrote. We assume that he lived after the Exile and opposed the exclusiveness of that period. We can see that he preferred a subtle but effective approach, rather than direct confrontation, to make his point. He was surely a person of great sensitivity.

He was also one of the world's greatest storytellers. Ruth contains scarcely a wasted word. The plot is clear and concise. The writer has spiced his story with small but significant human details and peopled it with skillfully drawn characters. He even takes care to use archaic language in the older people's dialogue. Suspense builds steadily toward the final resolution. Then our author neatly ties the story up with an all-around happy ending. This is the work of a real master!

Place in the Canon

Ruth was not originally part of the great Deuternomic history that encompasses most of Deuteronomy through 2 Kings. In the Hebrew Bible Ruth appears in the third section, among the Writings. Greek and Latin versions placed Ruth after Judges, probably because the story is set in the Judges period. Modern Bibles retain this later positioning.

Today, Jewish people read the book of Ruth during the feast of Weeks, an ancient celebration of the grain harvest.

Ruth 1–2

Introduction to These Chapters

Ruth's author moves quickly and directly into his story. In just five verses he sets the scene, introduces two or three main characters, and sets up the problem. In the remaining verses, he shows us more about the characters' personalities, leads us to identify with them, moves the plot along, and begins to hint at the possibility of a happy ending.

An outline of this section would include:
I.   Moab (1:1-18)
II. Bethlehem (1:19-22)
III. Gleaning (2:1-23)

Moab (1:1-18)

The story begins with a series of tragedies. First, there is a famine in Bethlehem. To find food, an Israelite family must move to the land of Moab. There the father dies, leaving his wife and two sons. The sons marry, but soon they, too die. That leaves three widows with no means of support. The two younger women could return to their families. Naomi, however, can only hope for help from distant relatives back in Bethlehem. As she prepares for the long, lonely journey home, Naomi urges her daughters-in-law to return to their parents. She prays, too, that the girls may find new husbands. Reluctantly, one young woman departs. Ruth, however, insists on going with Naomi. She is willing to leave her own family and nation to care for her aging mother-in-law. She knows that, in a foreign land, she will have few rights or protections and that her chances for remarriage are almost nil. She risks a life of loneliness and poverty to offer the gift of love.

The story is set rather vaguely in the Judges period (around 1200–1050 B.C.). This opening phrase might be likened to "A long time ago" or "Once upon a time."

Bethlehem means *house of bread*. The area was one of the richest grain producers in Israel. Famine there would be serious indeed.

Moab was a land on the southeastern side of the Dead Sea.

Elimelech means *God is King* or *the king is my God*.

Naomi means *delight, my joy*, or *sweet*.

Mahlon means *weakening*.

Chilion (Kilion) means *pining*.

The *Ephrathites* were a family group who lived in the settlement of Ephrathah, a section of Bethlehem.

The meaning of *Orpah* is uncertain. It probably is related to the word for cloud. If so, it would make a fine contrast with Ruth. Orpah is a cloud, but Ruth is a downpour.

Ruth means *water abundantly*. Ruth's kindness will make a dry and barren life bloom again.

Naomi has lost a great deal. She is alone with no means of support and no children. This last would be especially troubling. Ancient Hebrews did not believe in personal life after death. One's earthly life could continue, however, as it passed on into succeeding generations.

The LORD had considered his people (NRSV; NIV = *had come to the aid of his people*, verse 6): This is one of the few spots where Ruth's author shows God acting directly in the story's events.

Return to Judah (verse 7): The wording means *set out*

on the road to Judah. At this point Ruth and Orpah are merely accompanying Naomi for a short way.

If Mahlon and Chilion had had brothers, these brothers would have been required to marry Ruth and Orpah, support them, and have sons by them in their dead brothers' names. But there are no more brothers. Naomi is past child-bearing age and has no husband. Even if she should somehow have new sons, it would be many years before they could grow up and marry the young widows. Staying with Naomi is not a logical solution to Ruth's and Orpah's problems.

In her grief, Naomi accuses God of making her suffer. Much Old Testament thought assumes that God is directly responsible for everything that happens.

Orpah kissed her mother-in-law. We sense that Orpah, too, loves Naomi. She does not wrong or reject Naomi. She goes back home out of common sense, obedience, or both.

Ruth's well-known vow (verses 16-17) ends the women's discussion. To break the vow would call down God's wrath. Naomi can no longer ask Ruth to change her mind.

Note that, in adopting a new land, Ruth also adopts the God of that land. The author accepts Ruth's right to do this. In fact, throughout the story he presents Ruth as an ironic model of the true Israelite, a person living in godly kindness and responsibility.

Bethlehem (1:19-22)

Ruth and Naomi reach Bethlehem. The townspeople gather around to greet their old neighbor. Naomi explains what has happened and cries out in bitterness against God for all her suffering.

The author neatly brings this section to a close by noting that the women arrive during barley harvest. This subtly brings up the problem of food and sets the stage for the next episode.

The people *stirred,* or *hummed* like a warm of bees.

Mara means *bitter,* in contrast with Naomi's given name, which means *sweet* or *joy.*

The term *Moabitess* or the word *foreigner* is used many times to emphasize Ruth's origins.

The *barley harvest* usually takes place in late April.

Gleaning (2:1-23)

The women need food, so Ruth goes to glean. She begins working in a field that belongs to Boaz, a relative of Elimelech's. Boaz welcomes Ruth, gives her permission to glean, sees that she has food, water, and protection, and expresses appreciation for her kindness to Naomi. He even quietly instructs his field hands to leave some extra grain for Ruth to find. Boaz is obviously a kind, thoughtful person. We may even suspect that he is attracted to Ruth.

Ruth, for her part, puts in a hard day's work, takes home a good deal of grain, and even shares some of her luncheon leftovers with Naomi. By such detail the writer methodically builds up his picture of Ruth's goodness.

The meaning of *Boaz* is obscure. It may be *in him is strength.*

To *glean* is to pick up produce dropped in the harvest field. In Israel the poor had the right to glean, but that right did not extend to foreigners. Boaz offers Ruth kindness that is beyond what the law requires.

Was it really "luck" that brought Ruth to Boaz's field, or did God lead her there?

The use of the term *my daughter* suggests two things about Boaz: his age (he is much older than Ruth), and his gentle, fatherly concern for her.

Ruth risks several harassment or worse out in fields alone, so she is instructed to *keep close to my young women* (NRSV; NIV = *follow along after the girls*).

In verse 9, Boaz tells Ruth to drink water from vessels that have already been filled. The water would have to be carried to the field from the town well. Because of the extra work involved, Ruth needs permission to drink.

The quantity of an *ephah* is uncertain and may have changed over the centuries. Estimates range from two-thirds of a bushel to 29 pounds to 47.5 pounds. At any rate, it was apparently a good day's gleaning.

Naomi senses a possible solution to their problem and thanks God.

Boaz is related to Elimelech. This relationship may mean that Boaz has some legal rights or obligations to Naomi. In chapter 3 we will see that this legal situation provides the eventual solution to Ruth's and Naomi's problem.

The *wheat harvest* is in early June.

§ § § § § § §

The Message of Ruth 1–2

The message of these chapters is tied in with the message of the entire story. One part of that message is that righteous living—righteousness beyond the ordinary—brings happiness. Here we see the first steps in that process. Ruth has cared for Naomi. Now, in her need, Ruth has come to the field of an extraordinarily kind man. Moreover, this is a man in whom Naomi sees the possibility for more permanent help.

We also see here the beginnings of another message. Repeatedly the author reminds us that Ruth is a foreigner, and repeatedly we are shown that she is an unusually good person. Boaz, an obviously upright man, treats her with special kindness. Thus we learn that foreigners are not vile creatures to be avoided, but human beings with whom we can give and receive love.

These messages speak, not just to the past, but to our lives today. On a personal level, Ruth challenges us to live lives that go beyond the mediocrity of niceness. Through his story the author reminds us that real goodness is worth striving for. On both the personal and wider social levels, we who still live amidst racial prejudice and international suspicion need Ruth's second message. We need Ruth's reminder that surface differences do not negate our common humanity nor our capacity to share love.

§ § § § § § §

Ruth 3–4

Introduction to These Chapters

Now tension builds as the story moves through a series of hurdles to what listeners hope will be a happy ending. Naomi and Ruth take a large, but calculated risk; Boaz, though willing to help the women, must get by a legal obstacle. For a time, that legality nearly ruins the hoped-for solution. But, in the end, goodness triumphs, and "they all live happily ever after." Thus the writer skillfully develops his story to climax and resolution.

Someone, either the basic author or a later editor, has added a genealogy to the happy ending. The list follows Ruth's descendants down to King David. This information is not necessary to the plot but serves to underline the author's message that God accepts foreigners and that Israel should do so too. After all, if David had a Moabite great-grandmother, can Moabites be all that bad?

These chapters can be divided into three parts:
  I. Naomi's Plan (3:1-18)
 II. A Slight Hitch (4:1-12)
III. Conclusion (4:13-22)

Naomi's Plan (3:1-18)

Naomi outlines to Ruth a rather daring plan. Ruth is to fix herself up prettily, go to Boaz at night, and ask for his protection as a kinsman. The situation is a seductive one and not without dangers. Naomi is counting very heavily on Boaz's goodness.

Ruth approaches Boaz as Naomi has instructed. Boaz does prove to be as good a man as Naomi had hoped. He protects Ruth and agrees to help the women. He warns, however, that there is a stumbling block. Another man is a nearer relative than he. This other man has first right and obligation in the matter. Boaz must somehow get this man to forfeit his position.

Ruth returns home early in the morning when she can walk safely. At this time of the morning, however, it is still dark enough to protect both her own and Boaz's reputations. Boaz sends a gift for Naomi as a kindness and a sign of goodwill.

The author's flair for human detail is especially apparent in these verses. Naomi's plan is psychologically perfect. It appeals to the attraction we suspect Boaz feels for Ruth while also appealing, Naomi hopes, to his protective instinct. How can a good man refuse an attractive woman who obviously needs help, especially if he is already halfway in love with her?

Through the plan and its execution the author heightens the story's tension. Listeners know that Ruth is taking a big chance, and they hope that Boaz will be worthy of Naomi's trust. Then, while we are still sighing with relief that Ruth is all right, we learn of the nearer-kinsman obstacle. Naomi's admonition to "wait and see" is the perfect note for the author to close this chapter and draw listeners into the next. This writer definitely knows how to keep his audience on the edges of their seats!

Ancient Israelites separated the chaff from the grain by forking the grain up into a breeze and letting the wind blow the chaff away. Early evening was usually the best time for this. Boaz would have to stay through the night, however, to guard his grain from theft.

Uncover his feet (verse 4): This is a "loaded" expression.

The author may have used it intentionally, knowing that its ambiguity would increase the story's tension. *Feet* (or in some translations *legs*) is often used in the Old Testament as a euphemism for genital organs. It also can mean simply feet. How much does Naomi mean for Ruth to uncover? We learn shortly that Naomi does mean feet literally. Ruth is to carry out a symbolic act as part of her request for help. But the phrase's double meaning reminds listeners that this situation is fraught with temptation. Despite that temptation, these two good people will choose the best of behaviors.

In saying, *Spread your cloak* (NRSV; NIV = *corner of your garment*), Ruth is asking for Boaz's protection. The word *cloak* is translated in 2:12 as God's *wings*, the place where one finds shelter. Here it refers to a corner of Boaz's garment.

Boaz is delighted that Ruth has come to him. He recognizes that the kinsman's duty involves marrying her, and he has loved her for some time. He is much older than she, however, and perhaps has feared that she would want a younger husband. How thrilled he is to learn that she does not! Now he who was alone will also know the joy of marriage.

The word for *lie down (here)* is the word for *lodge*. It carries no sexual connotations. By using this word, the writer thus reassures us that, despite the circumstances, Boaz will act honorably.

A Slight Hitch (4:1-12)

Next morning Boaz begins legal action. To work things properly he must somehow deal with the nearer kinsman. Boaz assembles the town elders. He announces the sale of Naomi's land. The nearer kinsman has the first right and obligation for the land and for Naomi's care. The man, seeing his duty, agrees. But Boaz reminds him that the deal also includes Ruth. The man reconsiders. He has a family of his own. He would have to support Ruth and Naomi and have a son by Ruth. That son would inherit the land. Investing in this land would not do the man's own children any good. The whole package is going to be very expensive for him with little compensation in return. Boaz seems interested, so the man offers to relinquish his rights. Boaz gladly accepts them.

The *gate* was the place where the elders met to settle legal questions and other town affairs.

The kinsman—redeemer (NIV; NRSV = *next of kin*) remains unnamed. Perhaps the author is saying that this man's personality is not important to the story; only his status is. Did he come by chance? Had Boaz alerted him to come? Had God guided him there? The author does not say.

Ten men is the number needed for a marriage benediction. Boaz wants to be ready.

When Boaz mentions a *parcel (piece) of land,* it is the first time we hear of any land being involved. Ruth or Naomi may have spoken of it to Boaz, but the writer has not told us so. It is possible that Boaz himself remembered a piece of land and devised his plan around it.

The man would not be literally buying Ruth as a slave. Ruth does, however, go with the land as part of the kinsman's obligation.

Rachel and Leah were Jacob's wives, the mothers of all Israel.

All children after the first son would be credited to Boaz. He who had no son will now have many. Boaz's life will pass to another generation.

Conclusion (4:13-22)

Ruth and Boaz marry. They have a son who is credited to Mahlon. He is thus a grandson for Naomi. This child will eventually become the grandfather of Israel's greatest king, David.

Naomi again has a family and the joy of children. What's more she has a "descendant" to carry on her life and that of Elimelech.

The genealogy of verses 18-22 may be a later addition to the story. It emphasizes the fact that even David carried Moabite blood. Besides underlining acceptance of foreigners, this reference to David might have been an important factor in the book's inclusion among the sacred writings.

Note that the genealogy goes through Boaz rather than Mahlon. This may be a slip on the part of the genealogy writer or it may indicate some variations in traditions about David.

§ § § § § § §

The Message of Ruth 3–4

The book's double message carries through to its conclusion. Here, as in earlier chapters, we see that (1) goodness brings eventual happiness, and (2) God accepts other peoples and wants Israel to do the same. Underneath everything we see the hand of God caring for the people, leading them toward joy.

It is easy for modern Christians to be drawn into the selfishness, the mediocrity, the prejudice, and the cynicism of the world around us. A book like Ruth reminds us again that more-than-conventional goodness is worthwhile, that prejudice and exclusiveness are not God's ways, and that God really does care and work toward our happiness. We need that reminder. Thank God for giving it to us in this exquisite little story!

§ § § § § § §

Glossary of Terms

Abdon: A judge from Ephraim. He provided wise administration in time of peace.

Abimelech: A son of Gideon. Abimelech killed his brothers and set himself up as king of Shechem.

Achan: A man from the tribe of Judah who stole booty devoted to God. Achan's sin caused Joshua's army to lose in its first attempt to capture Ai.

Achor: A valley on the northern border of Judah. In this valley Joshua executed Achan for stealing booty from the defeated city of Jericho.

Achsah: The daughter of Caleb and wife of Othniel. Achsah asked for and received rights to a spring for Othniel's land in the Negeb.

Adonizedek: King of Jerusalem. Adonizedek led four other kings in opposing Joshua's conquest of Palestine. Joshua killed him at Makkedah.

Ai: "The ruin," a city near Bethel.

Amalekites: A nomadic tribe that ranged over the Palestine area.

Ammonites: A non-Israelite tribe living in the territory east of the Jordan.

Amorites: A non-Israelite tribe. Some Amorites lived in the area claimed by Judah; others lived east of the Jordan in Bashan and Heshbon.

Anakim: A tribe, described as giants, that inhabited Canaan before the Israelite conquest. Anakim are usually connected with southern sites.

Angel: A messenger of God.

Arabah: The Jordan Valley. The Arabah may also include the Dead Sea and the area from the Dead Sea to the Gulf of Aqabah.

Ark of the Covenant: Sacred box holding the law. The ark represented God's powerful presence among the people.

Asher: One of the twelve tribes of Israel. Asher settled in the north near the seacoast.

Asherah: A Semitic goddess or a cult object related to her worship. The King James Version mistranslates the term as "grove."

Ashkelon: A Philistine city located on the Mediterranean seacoast.

Astarte/Ashtoreth (pl. *Ashtaroth):* A Canaanite goddess used in worship rituals.

Azekah: A city in southern Palestine about fifteen miles northwest of Hebron. Here a rain of hailstones helped Joshua defeat Adonizedek's forces.

Baal: A Canaanite god.

Ban: A decree requiring absolute destruction of everything in a conquered city.

Barak: A judge who, with Deborah, led Israel in defeating Sisera.

Bashan: Amorite territory east of the Jordan and well to the north.

Benjamin: One of the twelve tribes of Israel. Benjamin's territory was in southern Palestine in the territory north of the Dead Sea.

Bethel: A city in central Palestine. Early in the Judges period the ark of the covenant was at Bethel.

Bethlehem: (1) A city south of Jerusalem, original home of Micah's Levite, of the Ephraimite Levites concubine, and of Naomi and Boaz. (2) A town of the same name to the north, in Zebulun.

Beth-millo: A fortress at Shechem.

Boaz: Ruth's protector and second husband.

Caleb: One of the spies who entered Canaan before the Israelite conquest. In the land division he received the city of Hebron.

Canaan: Palestine west of the Jordan extending into the coast of Syria.

Canaanites: Non-Israelites who inhabited Palestine.

Chemosh: A Moabite god.

Chilion (Kilion): Naomi's son, Orpah's husband.

Chinnereth, Chinneroth: Sea of Galilee.

Circumcise: To remove the foreskin from the male genital

organ. In Israel, circumcision was a sign of dedication to God and membership in God's people.

Conquest: The period (thirteenth century B.C.) when Israel entered Palestine and took possession of the land.

Covenant: A sacred agreement.

Cubit: About eighteen inches.

Cushan-rishathaim: King of Aram-naharaim, the first oppressor in the Book of Judges. He was defeated by the Israelite judge Othniel.

D: Any biblical writer or editor of the Deuteronomic school. D writers were especially active around the time of King Josiah (7th century B.C.) and after the Exile (587–538 B.C.). Joshua and Judges are D works.

Dagon: A Philistine god.

Dan: One of the twelve tribes of Israel. Dan first settled in the southern plains, then moved to the far north.

Debir: A city in southern Palestine; also, the king of Eglon who joined in a coalition opposing Joshua.

Deborah: A judge who united several tribes of Israel to defeat their Canaanite oppressors.

Delilah: Philistine woman who led Samson into slavery.

Deuteronomic: Referring to a literary group and its common theological outlook. The Deuteronomists produced a lengthy history of Israel, including the books of Deuteronomy, Joshua, and Judges.

Ebal: A mountain near Shechem situated opposite Mount Gerizim.

Eglon: A city in southern Palestine whose king opposed Joshua; also, the Moabite king whom Ehud killed.

Ehud: A Benjaminite hero who stabbed the oppressive Moabite king, Eglon.

Eleazar: A priest at the time of Joshua.

Elimelech: Naomi's husband.

Elon: A minor judge from Zebulun.

Ephah: A unit of measure whose value is now uncertain. Various estimates give it 2/3 bushel, 29 pounds, and 47.5 pounds.

Ephod: A priestly garment.

Ephraim: Son of Joseph and one of the twelve tribes of Israel. When Joshua divided the land, the priestly tribe of Levi received no portion, but Joseph received two, one for Ephraim and one for Manasseh. Thus there were still twelve territorial divisions. Ephraim's land was in the hill country of central Palestine.

Exile: Period from the Fall of Jerusalem (587 B.C.) to the Jews' release (538 B.C.). During this time many of Israel's people lived as captives in Babylon.

Exodus: The escape of Moses and the Hebrews from oppression in Egypt.

Gaal: The man who turned the people of the city of Shechem against Abimelech.

Gad: One of the twelve tribes. Gad settled in the territory east of the Jordan.

Gate: Entrance to a walled city and public gathering place. In ancient Israel, the elders sat at the city gate to carry out legal activities.

Gaza: A Philistine city near the southern coast.

Gerizim: A mountain near Shechem situated opposite Mount Ebal.

Gezer: A city in the Palestinian plain.

Gibeah: The inhospitable Benjaminite city whose men killed a traveling Levite's concubine and provoked a war.

Gibeon: A city six miles northwest of Jerusalem whose people made a treaty with Joshua.

Gideon: Judge from Manasseh who rid Israel of Midianite oppression. He is known for panicking the enemy army with sudden torchlight, noise, and victory shouts.

Gilead: A large area east of the Jordan.

Gilgal: A city close to the Jordan near Jericho. Gilgal was Israel's main base during the conquest.

Girgashites: A non-Israelite tribe living in Palestine.

Glean: To pick up leftover produce in a harvest field.

Great Sea: The Mediterranean.

Hazor: A Canaanite city in the north whose king opposed Joshua. In Deborah's time, Hazor was a center of Canaanite oppression.

Hebron: A city nineteen miles south of Jerusalem. The Anakim occupied Hebron until Caleb captured it.

Hittites: A people from the north who maintained a vast Middle-eastern empire before the time of Israel's conquest of Palestine.

Hivites: A people living in Canaan before the Israelite conquest. The name is sometimes interchanged with *Horites.*

Hoham: King of Hebron who opposed Joshua.

Horites: Hurrians dwelling in Palestine, sometimes called *Hivites.*

Ibzan: A minor judge from the border between Asher and Zebulun. He administered his area in time of peace.

Jabesh-gilead: A city east of the Jordan which did not participate in the Benjaminite war. As punishment, its people were killed except for 400 virgins who were given to the surviving Benjaminites.

Jabin: King of Hazor who opposed Joshua; also one of the oppressors against whom Deborah revolted.

Jael: Woman who murdered Sisera as he fled from Deborah and Barak's troops.

Jair: Minor judge from Gilead who administered his territory in peacetime.

Japhia: King of Lachish who joined in a coalition to oppose Joshua.

Jarmuth: A city in Judah which opposed Joshua's invasion.

Jashar, Book of: An ancient book of poetry containing Joshua's address to the sun and moon.

Jebusites: Canaanite tribe that occupied the city of Jebus (Jerusalem).

Jephthah: Judge from Gilead who rid Israel of invading Ammonites and sacrificed his daughter to fulfill a vow.

Jephunneh: Caleb's father.

Jericho: A city near the west bank of the Jordan, sometimes called the "city of palms." Jericho was the first city Joshua captured.

Jerubaal: Another name for Gideon.

Jezreel: A town in Issachar at the foot of Mount Gilboa; a plain and a valley near the town.

Joash: Gideon's father.

Jordan: The river that runs north and south along the mountainous spine of Palestine.

Joshua: Moses' successor, the general who led Israel in its conquest and settlement of Palestine.

Jotham: Son of Gideon who survived Abimelech's slaughter and spoke out against Abimelech's coronation as king of Shechem.

Judah: One of the twelve tribes of Israel. Judah settled in the south of Palestine.

Judges: (1) Charismatic persons who gave Israel military and administrative leadership before Israel had a king; (2) the time when the judges ruled (approximately 1200–1050 B.C.); (3) the biblical book that tells the stories of the judges.

Kadesh-barnea: A town south of Israel where the Hebrews stayed after leaving Mount Sinai.

Kedesh: Barak's home in eastern Galilee. Deborah and Barak mustered their troops there.

Kenaz: An Edomite clan chief, ancestor of the Kenizites; Othniel's father.

Kenites: Semi-nomadic people living in the territory south of Palestine.

Kenizites: An Edomite tribe living in southern Judah and the Negeb. Caleb and Othniel were Kenizites.

Kinsman: A relative. The nearest kinsman had the first right to purchase a relative's land. He also had certain obligations toward his relative's widow.

Kiriath-arba: Ancient name for Debir.

Kishon: A stream running from the Palestinian hills to the sea.

Lachish: A city in Judah midway between Jerusalem and Gaza.

Laish: Canaanite city in northern Palestine later known as Dan.

Lebanon: A mountain range located in the area to the north of Palestine.

Lehi: "The jawbone," a place between Zorah and Timnah where Samson fought the Philistines.

Levi: One of the tribes of Israel. The men of Levi were set aside to serve as priests. In the land division, Levi did not receive a territorial inheritance. Instead the Levites were assigned certain cities spread throughout Palestine.

Levite: A priest, a member of the tribe of Levi.

Machir: A clan of Manasseh. Some texts locate Machir east of the Jordan, others to the west.

Madon: A Canaanite town in Galilee that joined Jabin's confederation against Joshua.

Mahaneh-dan: Camp of Dan, a place located to the west of Kiriath-jearim.

Mahlon: Naomi's son, Ruth's first husband.

Makkedah: A Canaanite city near which Joshua trapped five kings in a cave.

Manasseh: Son of Joseph and one of the twelve tribes of Israel. Manasseh claimed territory on both sides of the Jordan.

Megiddo: A city overlooking the Valley of Jezreel in central Palestine.

Merom: A stream in Upper Galilee.

Mesopotamia: The area between the Tigris and Euphrates rivers far to the east of Palestine.

Micah: An Ephraimite from whom the Danites took religious objects and a priest.

Midianites: A nomadic tribe living to the south and east of Palestine.

Mizpah: A town in Benjamin; a town in Gilead; a town in Judah; a town in Moab; a valley located in the territory to the north of Palestine.

Moab: A land east of the Dead Sea. Israel camped in Moab before entering the Promised Land. Ruth was originally from Moab.

Naomi: Ruth's mother-in-law.

Naphtali: One of the twelve tribes of Israel. Naphtali settled on the west side of the Jordan in Galilee.

Nazirite: A person specially dedicated to God. The period of dedication could be temporary or life-long. Some Nazirites were designated by God; others chose to dedicate themselves. Later Nazirites distinguished themselves by abstaining from alcohol, by not cutting their hair, and by avoiding contact with the dead. However, earlier accounts do not include the third restriction.

Negeb: An arid area on the southern edge of Palestine.

Ophrah: Gideon's hometown in Manasseh.

Orpah: Naomi's daughter-in-law. After her husband died, Orpah chose to return to her family while Ruth vowed to remain forever with Naomi.

Othniel: The first deliverer listed in the Book of Judges. Othniel was an Edomite who became a part of the Israelite tribe of Judah. A kinsman of Caleb, Othniel captured Debir during the conquest and married Caleb's daughter. Later he rid Israel of the oppressor Cushan-rishathaim.

Penuel: A city on the east side of the Jordan. Gideon killed its inhabitants for refusing to help him.

Peor: A mountain in Moab.

Perizzites: Non-Israelites living in Canaan.

Philistines: Canaanite people who lived along the southern coast of the Mediterranean. During the Judges period they sometimes pushed inland, squeezing the Israelite tribes settled there.

Phinehas: The priest who settled the problem of an altar built by the eastern tribes.

Piram: King of Jarmuth who opposed Joshua's invasion.

Pisgah: A mountain in Moab across the Jordan from Jericho.

Rahab: A prostitute who sheltered the spies Joshua sent to Jericho.

Rephaim: Early inhabitants of Palestine described as giants; also a valley near Jerusalem.

Reuben: One of the twelve tribes of Israel. Reuben occupied land east of the Jordan.

Ruth: (1) A four-chapter short story which follows the Book of Judges; (2) the main figure in that story, a Moabite woman whose love and loyalty to her Israelite mother-in-law gave her a special place in God's chosen people.

Samson: An extremely strong man whom God used to punish Israel's Philistine oppressors.

Shamgar: A judge who killed large numbers of Philistines.

Shechem: An ancient Canaanite city in Ephraim, later an important Israelite center.

Shiloh: An important Israelite worship center located in Ephraim.

Shittim: A place in the plains of Moab, Israel's last campsite before crossing the Jordan.

Sidon: A Phoenician coastal city.

Simeon: One of the twelve tribes of Israel. Simeon occupied land in the far south of Palestine.

Succoth: A city east of the Jordan which Gideon punished for failing to help him.

Taanach: A city in Manasseh, one site for the battle between Sisera and Barak.

Tabor: A mountain in the Valley of Jezreel.

Teraphim: One or more idols.

Thebez: A town near Shechem attacked by Abimelech.

Theology: Understanding of God, study or discussion about God.

Timnah: A town on the northern border of Judah, home of Samson's wife.

Timnath-heres (Timnath-serah): Joshua's city.

Tola: A minor judge from Issachar.

Transjordanian tribes: The tribes of Reuben, Gad, and half of Manasseh which settled east of the Jordan.

Urim and Thummim: Sacred lots, a way of determining the will of God.

Zebulun: One of the twelve tribes of Israel. Zebulun occupied land in north-central Palestine.

Guide to Pronunciation

Abdon: AB-dun
Abimelech: Ah-BIH-meh-lek
Abinoam: Ah-bih-NOH-um
Achan: AH-kun
Achor: Ah-CORE
Achsah: AHK-sah
Achshaph: AHK-shahf
Adonizedek: Ah-doh-nigh-ZEH-dek
Ai: EYE
Aijalon: AY-jah-lon
Amalekites: Ah-MAL-eh-kites
Anakim: Ah-nah-KEEM
Aphek: AY-fek
Arabah: AR-ah-bah
Arad: AIR-ad
Aroer: Ah-ROH-er
Asherah: AH-sheh-rah
Ashtaroth: Ash-teh-ROTHE
Astarte: Ah-START
Azekah: Ah-zeh-KAH
Baal: Bah-ALL
Barak: Bah-RAK
Bashan: Bah-SHAHN
Bethhoron: Beth-HOR-un
Bethjeshimoth: Beth-jeh-shih-MOTHE
Boaz: BO-az
Bochim: Boh-KEEM
Chemosh: Keh-MOSH

Chilion: KIL-ee-un
Chinnereth: KIH-neh-reth
Cushan-rishathaim: KOO-shan-rish-uh-THAY-im
Debir: Deh-BEER
Edrei: EH-dreh-eye
Ehud: EE-hude
Eleazar: Eh-lee-AY-zar
Elimelech: Eh-lee-MEH-lek
Elon: EE-lon
Enhakkore: En-hah-KORE
Ephah: EE-fah
Ephod: EE-fod
Ephraim: EE-frah-eem
Eshtaol: ESH-tah-ole
Gaal: Gah-ALL
Gezer: GEH-zer
Gibeah: GIH-bee-ah
Gideon: GIH-dee-un
Gilead: GIH-lee-ad
Gilgal: GIL-gal
Goiim: Goh-EEM
Harosheth-ha-goiim: Hah-roh-SHETH-hah-goh-EEM
Hinnom: Hih-NOME
Hittites: HIT-ites
Jabesh-gilead: Jah-besh-GIH-lee-ad
Jabin: JAY-bin
Jael: Jah-ELL
Jair: Jah-EER
Jashar: Jah-SHAHR
Jebus: JEH-bus
Jebusite: JEB-you-site
Jephthah: JEF-thah
Jericho: JEH-rih-koh
Jerubaal: Jeh-ROO-bah-all
Jephunneh: Jeh-FOO-neh
Jezreel: JEZ-reh-eel
Joash: JO-ash
Jokneam: Joke-NEE-um

Jotham: JOH-thum
Kadesh-barnea: Kah-desh-bar-NEE-uh
Kedesh: KEH-desh
Kenaz: KEH-naz
Kenites: KEH-nites
Kenizzites: KEH-nih-zites
Kiriath-arba: Kir-ee-ath-AR-buh
Kiriath-sepher: Kir-ee-ath-SAY-fer
Kishon: KEE-shon
Lachish: Lah-KEESH
Laish: Lah-EESH
Lasharon: Lah-shah-RONE
Lehi: LEE-high
Levite: LEE-vite
Libnah: LIB-nuh
Machir: Mah-KEER
Madon: Mah-DON
Mahlon: Mah-LON
Makkedah: Mah-kay-DAH
Manasseh: Muh-NASS-eh
Megiddo: Meh-GID-oh
Merom: Mare-OME
Micah: MY-cuh
Misrephoth-maim: MIZ-reh-foth-mah-EEM
Midianites: MID-ee-uh-nites
Moab: MOH-ab
Naomi: Nay-OH-mee
Naphath-dor: Nah-fath-DOR
Naphtali: Naf-TAL-lee
Negeb: NEH-geb
Orpah: OR-puh
Penuel: PEN-yoo-el
Peor: Peh-ORE
Perizzites: PER-iz-ites
Philistines: FIH-liss-teens
Pisgah: PIZ-guh
Rahab: RAY-hab
Rephaim: Reh-fah-EEM

Salecah: Sah-leh-KAH
Shechem: SHEK-um
Shiloh: SHY-low
Shimron-meron: Shim-RONE-meer-OWN
Shittim: Shih-TEEM
Succoth: SUH-cuth
Taanach: Tah-ah-NAHK
Tappuah: Tah-POO-uh
Teraphim: Teh-rah-FEEM
Thebez: THEH-bez
Thummim: THUM-im
Timnah: Tim-NAH
Timnath-serah: Tim-nath-seh-RAH
Tola: TOH-lah
Urim: YOOR-im
Zebulun: ZEB-yoo-lun

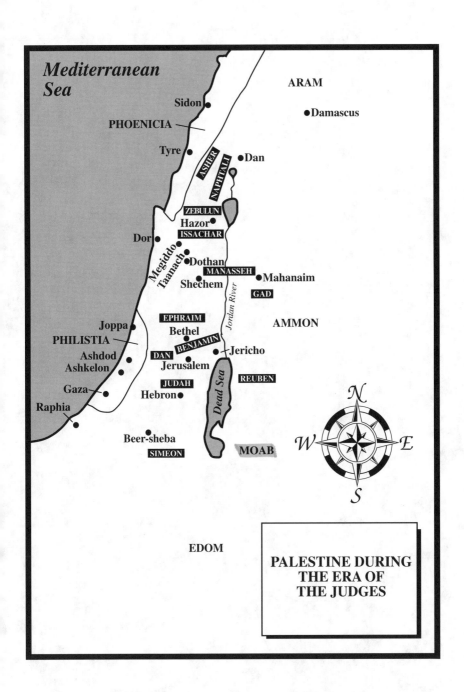

PALESTINE DURING
THE ERA OF
THE JUDGES